# 60 SECONDS TO

## VOLUME 3

## 101 ORIGINAL ONE-MINUTE MONOLOGUES
### BY GLENN ALTERMAN

MONOLOGUE AUDITION SERIES

**A Smith and Kraus Book**

Published by Smith and Kraus, Inc.
177 Lyme Road, Hanover, NH 03755
www.SmithandKraus.com

First Edition: February 2006
9 8 7 6 5 4 3 2 1
Cover and text design by Julia Hill Gignoux
Author photo by Robert Kim

The Monologue Audition Series   ISSN 1067-134X
Cataloging-in-Publication Data

Alterman, Glenn, 1964–
60 seconds to shine. Volume 3, 101 one-minute monologues / by Glenn Alterman.
    p. cm. — (Monologue audition series)
ISBN 1-57525-431-X / ISBN-13 978-1-57525-431-9
1. Monologues. 2. Acting. 3. Acting—Auditions. I. Title: 101 one-minute
monologues. II. Title: Sixty seconds to shine. III. Title: One hundred one one-
minute monologues. IV. Title: One hundred and one one-minute monologues. V.
Title. VI. Series.

PN2080.A4418 2005
812'.54dc22
             2005054139

NOTE: These monologues are intended to be used for audition and class
study; permission is not required to use the material for those purposes.
However, if there is a paid performance of any of the monologues in-
cluded in this book, please contact the publisher for permission information.

# THE AUTHOR

GLENN ALTERMAN is the author of *The Perfect Audition Monologue, Street Talk (Original Character Monologues for Actors.), Two Minutes and Under (Volumes 1, 2, and 3), Uptown, Two-Minute Monologs, Creating Your Own Monologue, The Job Book: One Hundred Acting Jobs for Actors, The Job Book 2: One Hundred Day Jobs for Actors, What to Give Your Agent for Christmas, An Actor's Guide: Making It in New York City,* and the recently revised *Promoting Your Acting Career: A Step by Step Program to Opening Doors.*

*Two Minutes and Under (Volumes 1 and 2), Street Talk, Uptown, Creating Your Own Monologue, Promoting Your Acting Career, The Job Book, The Job Book 2,* and *An Actor's Guide: Making It in New York City* were all "Featured Selections" in the Doubleday Book Club (Fireside Theater and Stage and Screen Division). Most of his published works have gone on to multiple printings.

Alterman wrote the book for *Heartstrings: The National Tour* (commissioned by the Design Industries Foundation for Aids), a thirty-five city tour that starred Michelle Pfeiffer, Ron Silver, Christopher Reeve, Susan Sarandon, Marlo Thomas, and Sandy Duncan. His recent book, *The Perfect Audition Monologue,* was honored by the National Arts Club in New York City.

Alterman's plays *Like Family* and *The Pecking Order* were optioned by Red Eye Films (with Alterman writing the screenplay). His latest play, *Solace,* was produced Off-Broadway by Circle East Theater Company and presently has several European productions. *Solace* was recently optioned for European TV. *Nobody's Flood* won the Bloomington National Playwriting Competition as well as being a finalist in The Key West Playwriting Competition. *Coulda-Woulda-Shoulda* twice won the Three Genres Playwriting Competition and was published in two separate editions of the Prentice Hall college textbook. It has received several New York productions.

Other plays include *Kiss Me When It's Over* (commissioned by E. Weissman Productions), starring and directed by Andre DeShields; *Tourists of the Mindfield* (finalist in the L. Arnold Weissberger Playwriting Competition at New Dramatists); and *Street*

*Talk/Uptown* (based on his monologue books), produced at The West Coast Ensemble.

*Goin' Round on Rock Solid Ground, Unfamiliar Faces,* and *Words Unspoken* were all finalists at the Actor's Theater of Louisville. *Spilt Milk* received its premiere at the Beverly Hills Rep/Theater 40 in Los Angeles and was selected to participate in The Samuel French One-Act Festival on two separate occasions. It's had over thirty productions. *The Danger of Strangers* won Honorable Mention in both The Deep South Writers Conference Competition and the Pittsburgh New Works Festival and was also a finalist in the George R. Kernodle Contest. There have been over twenty productions, including The West Bank Downstairs Theater production, which starred James Gandolphini. His work has been performed at Primary Stages, Circle in the Square Downtown, The Turnip Festival, HERE theater, LaMama, the Duplex, Playwrights Horizons, and at several theaters on Theater Row in New York, as well as at many other theaters around the country.

He is one of the country's foremost monologue and audition coaches, having helped thousands of actors in their search for (and preparation of) monologues, as well as creating their own material for solo shows. Glenn has lectured and taught at such diverse places as The Edward Albee Theater Conference (Valdez, Alaska), Southampton College, Governors School For the Arts (Old Dominion University), The School for Film and Television, Western Connecticut State College, Star Map Acting School of Long Island, the Dramatists Guild, The Learning Annex, The Screen Actors Guild, The Seminar Center, Emblazon Productions, and Broadway's Artists Alliance and in the Boston public school system, as well as at many acting schools all over the country. In 1994 he created The Glenn Alterman Studio (www.glennalterman.com), and through its auspices he has worked privately as a monologue and audition coach and at colleges, universities, and acting schools all around the country.

Alterman presently lives in New York City where he is working on a new commissioned play, completing a screenplay, coaching actors, giving seminars, and occasionally working in film and TV.

# CONTENTS

## MEN'S MONOLOGUES

## WOMEN'S MONOLOGUES

# INTRODUCTION

When my publisher, Eric Kraus, first suggested my writing a book of 101 one-minute monologues, I had a mixed response. Half of me felt that this could be the easiest book of monologues I've ever written, and the other half felt that it could be the most difficult. Well I was right, on both counts. As actors, I'm sure you're aware, that one minute of dialogue is short; *very short*! It's almost over before it begins. So the real task in working on these monologues would be to try to fit a character, a situation, an emotional arc, a beginning, middle, and end, and possibly even a conflict all into one minute. We're talking instant character, engaging dialogue, and a situation that resolves itself almost immediately. Instant, instant everything! And add to that, there had to be 101 totally different stories with 101 different characters of all ages, types, and social levels. Well, I love a good challenge. And there was no doubt, working on this book would be an immense challenge. I agreed to do it.

Audition monologues are first and foremost, marketing tools whose only purpose is to help you get an agent, win an audition, or showcase your acting skills to theater companies, directors, and producers. Monologues are an invaluable part of every actors' marketing arsenal. Just as you must have an up-to-date picture and résumé, you should have at least four (or more) well-rehearsed, ready-to-go monologues in your arsenal. One question you must always ask yourself before selecting any monologue is, "What is it I want them to see (know) about me as an actor?" The monologue you select should reveal to the auditors the best of what you have to offer at this time in your career. I find that most actors pick a monologue because they like the character or dialogue, or what the character in the monologue is saying. While these are certainly very important factors, they shouldn't be the only reasons you choose a specific monologue. This is one of the rare times in your acting career where *you* get to choose the material you'll be performing. Aside from showcasing your talent, the monologue reflects your personal taste, your aesthetic. Remember, this is the first impression that the auditors will have of you as an actor (and as a person). Be selective; don't make quick decisions. This is too important. If you'd like to learn more about how to prepare for monologue auditions, please get a copy of my book, *The Perfect Audition Monologue* (Smith and Kraus). In that book I discuss in detail how you should select and work on new material. There's also a long chapter of interviews with casting directors and agents discussing what they look for at monologue auditions.

What I suggest is that you first look through the contents of this book. I've listed the monologues by their character names, age range, whether they are comedic or dramatic (or seriocomedic), and a quick reference as to what the monologue is about. I wouldn't be too concerned about the age that's listed for each character. Age is arbitrary, and you may find a monologue that you like but notice that the age listed might be a little older or younger than you. I say go for it.

After you select the monologues that interest you, read through them. If you decide you like one, read it again, but this time read it out loud. If the words feel comfortable and you feel a connection to the character, you may have a keeper. Don't limit yourself. As I mentioned, you should have an arsenal of monologues ready for auditions. You should constantly replenish stale material with new ones that excite you. The excitement you feel about new material often translates into enthusiasm in the audition room. And if there's one thing, aside from talent, that auditors are looking for, it's enthusiasm.

Trust your instincts. If you personally identify with the character, what he or she is saying, what his or her situation is, working on that character, personalizing the monologue, will be a lot easier. This is not the time to *stretch*. If you want to use new acting muscles, take a scene study class.

Many casting directors have an incredible memory. Don't be surprised if you happen to meet one ten years after you've auditioned for them, and they're able to call you by your first name. They remember, so make your auditions memorable. I strongly believe you should never waste an audition trying out new material. Every audition is important. You never know where that casting director, agent, or director will end up down the road.

You'll notice there are many monologues in this book that are topical. Taking a cue from the *Law and Order* TV shows, I realized that every day there are dramatic and humorous stories in the news. Quite a few characters in this book have stories that will seem very current. There's Vivian, an *American Idol* contestant; Bette, a runaway bride; Maureen, whose mom left their family to go to Rome to attend the pope's funeral; and Jack, an army sergeant in Iraq confronting a traitor soldier, among others.

In addition to the 101 one-minute monologues, you'll find, as a bonus, a slew of one-and-a-half- and two-minute monologues. Some stories just couldn't be confined to one minute no matter how hard I tried.

I hope you'll find many monologues in this book that you'll want to use. I honestly believe there's something here for every actor, no matter what his or her type or taste.

I'd like to thank the many actors who participated in the workshops that we held to develop these monologues. I'd also like to thank my students who worked on developing some of these monologues as part of our work together. I'd especially like to express my appreciation to the casting directors and agents who took the time to read through the manuscript of this book and make invaluable comments. And finally, I'd like to thank all of you who have bought my previous books and took the time to write to me. Like actors, writers like to know that their work is appreciated.

I hope you'll find that *perfect* audition monologue in this book. There certainly are many to choose from. Maybe one of the monologues in this book will be the one that gets you that agent or job that is the springboard to a successful career.

Best of luck,
Glenn Alterman

# DEDICATION

I dedicate this book to all the actors, casting directors, and agents who have been so helpful with this book and all of my previous books. It's all about collaboration, and I couldn't have done it without all of you. Much thanks to everyone.

# ACKNOWLEDGMENTS

To Ana Traina, Mary Joy, and the casting directors and agents who took the time to read the manuscript for this book and give me invaluable comments.

To my students who were instrumental in helping me shape and rewrite these monologues: Susan Moses, Leslie Gail, Rick Marx, Gregory Waller, Donald Flores, Jeff House, Jim Beaudin, Mark Philip Jackson, Paul Krasner, Traci Skoldberg, Ross Laurence, Brain Schneider, Annie Patterson, Hillary Parker, Amy Milano, Chris Papandrea, Darryl Brown, Alicia Bowling, Jack Caputo, Ann Christiane Moller, Steve Grodewald, Christopher Byron Currie, Jeremy Redleaf, Jesse Kearney, Christopher Marchese, Angelica Bluewolf, Seth Welnick, Bobby Holder, Heather Aldridge, Ramon Villa, Judy Rosenblatt, Robin Gunning, Jordan Valdez, Nadia Jordan, Patrick O'Connor, Anne Nadell, Adam Montanaro, Patricia Cardello, and Mark Malick

# FRANK

30s

comedic

*Frank tries to talk his mom into turning his brother in for a reward.*

All we gotta do, all we gotta do is tell him we wanna go for a ride, a little ride, that's all. Tell him we're gonna go to the mall, Ma. That we wanna go shopping. You know how Tommy loves to shop. Tell him we wanna get some nice new T-shirts. And then when we get him in the car, we'll talk a lot, keep him talkin'. Then I'll turn the radio up real loud. And when he's not lookin', I'll hit him on the head. I won't hurt him, no, just knock him out. I mean he's my brother, I love the guy. I'll just knock him out a little, that's all. And then we'll bring him in, get the money. All that money, Ma, think about it. We could go to Puerto Rico or Jamaica. Sit in the sun and drink pina coladas and margaritas around a swimming pool. And all we gotta do is just get him in the car, knock him out, bring him to the cops. And we'll visit him, I swear, every month. And Tommy'll know we only did it for the money, was nothing personal. So go ahead, go ahead Ma, go wake him up. You wake him, and I'll go start the car.

# CHARLIE
30s to 50s
comedic

*Charlie, a loner, talks about his love
of animals.*

Basically, I just don't like people. Don't like 'em or trust 'em, that's all. People are just too selfish. Give me animals any day. Hey, I'm not saying animals don't have their flaws, but if you feed 'em, they'll stay faithful. But people, no matter how hard you try, sooner or later they'll stab you in the back. And no matter how much you love 'em, they'll leave you. That's been my experience. And that's why I'm perfectly content right here in my animal paradise. I feed 'em, take care of 'em, and they love me much more than either of my two bitch wives who ran off and stole almost all my money. But I'm not bitter, no, I'm a forgivin' man, I am. Let bygones be bygones. So I bought me this farm, got me these animals. And now I'm as happy as a pig in shit. Even got one, yeah, a pig. Named her Nina, after my second wife. And I got twelve terrific dogs, three adorable cats, eight furry, feisty gerbils, one overfriendly boa constrictor, eight playful little sheep, a parrot that can say "I love you," in both English and French, a hamster, eight hens, and, of course, a horse.

# BEN

20s to 30s
dramatic

*Ben recalls the last time he saw his girlfriend.*

Told her I was gonna go for a little jog. Said she'd wait
for me there on the beach. She looked so great in that
new blue bathing suit. A quick kiss, last look, and I was
off. Was one of those great days when the air and the
ocean . . . Beautiful. I was just getting a good pace going,
was looking out at the ocean. At first I thought maybe it
was the just the glare of the sun. It looked . . . looked like
there was a mountain in the middle of the ocean. I
stopped, rubbed my eyes. Seemed like it was getting
larger, was moving in toward the beach—fast. This huge
dark mountain! I turned toward where Tonya was down
the beach. Started screaming to her, but there was this in-
credibly loud sound from the ocean! I yelled, GET OFF
THE BEACH! But it was like my voice didn't have any
sound. Was like I was in a nightmare. I saw her just
standing there, way down the beach, she looked stunned.
She had seen it, but couldn't move. People on the beach
were frozen, screaming! But it was that sound, and the
sight of the mountain coming toward us. THE ROAR;
THE ROAR! And THEN IT CAME, THE WAVE, THE
WATER! *(A beat, very softly.)* I remember . . . remember
the first time she mentioned it, Sri Lanka. I said, "Sri
Lanka, isn't that a bit exotic?" "Oh come on, be brave
Ben. Let's be daring, have an adventure," she said. I could
see she really wanted to go. I kissed her, said "Sure,
why not?" Why not? I remember how great she looked
on the beach that day, in her new blue bathing suit. Her
smile . . . Beautiful.

# NED

50s to 70s

dramatic

*Ned talks about the patients who come to his clinic in the jungle.*

They come here, hoping. They track me down, travel far to find me. They come here to the middle of the jungle to see me—"the miracle man." And I look in their terrified eyes and tell them, "It's going to be okay." I give them a look of calm and a smile of unspoken reassurance. And their first night here they sleep better than they've slept in months, maybe years. And they dream of a tomorrow when all their pain will be gone, and they'll be cured. When they can go home, and life will be just like before. *(A beat.)* But there is no cure, of course not. All I have to offer is a painless and picturesque demise, here in the jungle. I feed them wonderful drugs to take away their anguish, as they drift in and out, see the sandman and smile. I'm sort of like Santa, but I carry hope instead of toys. I give them much more than just a cure. And each night before they go to what might be their last sleep, I give each and every one of them a gentle kiss on the cheek. And I whisper to them that they are loved; deeply, unconditionally loved.

# RON

30s to 40s

comedic

*A guy who just had a strange encounter
at a bar.*

So I go up to the bar, and there's this drop-dead gorgeous girl. Let's call her Elaine, she never gave me her name. Anyway, Elaine gives me *the* look. Pant, pant, I'm a puppy in heat. I'd just come from the office Christmas party, was a little loaded, stopped off at this bar for a nightcap. And so we start talking, and she's saying things I want to hear. I mean *things*! Nothing dirty, nothing raunchy, but . . . So I'm thinking maybe she's a pro, you know? So I ask her, and she gets really offended. I apologize, buy her a drink. Well, several drinks later, I'm in love, but my mind's in the gutter; and all I can think is where's my rubber. Soon I ask her if she'd like to leave. She says "Sure." BINGO! But when she stands up I notice Elaine is *tall*, I mean maybe six foot three. I look around and notice that in this bar there's only men, many, many men. Well, one plus one is two, and I ask her, and she says "I thought you knew." I said, "No, I had no idea." Man, what a drag. And so I leave, yeah, alone, as Elaine smiles, waving from the window.

# HOWARD

20s to 40s
dramatic

*Howard recalls a moment when he thought
he was going to be mugged.*

Maybe I'm a coward, I don't know. All I knew is when I saw them coming toward me, I wanted to run, fast. All I could imagine was the morning headline, "Man Murdered in Park." It was dark, and I had decided to take a shortcut. They were coming toward me. I could hear the hip-hop on their boom box, as they got closer and closer. Then their darkened silhouettes, shadows taking shape. I wanted to disappear, disintegrate. Danger! Then there they were, right in front of me. I smiled, as if to say, "Hey man, I'm not afraid." But I neither stopped nor stared. Faces, eyes, we saw each other. And then I continued walking, just floated by. And as quickly as they came, they went. As if . . . as if they weren't even there. Then I began to wonder, were they . . . were they there? Or was I just . . . ? It was dark, I left the park. Streetlights, cars, people. Safe. Of course. Of course. What the hell was I thinking?

# JOHN
30s to 40s
dramatic

*A lawyer talks of a prisoner sent to jail for a crime he didn't commit.*

You have any idea what it must feel like? I mean he did nothing wrong, this man, nothing! And because of some unprepared court-appointed lawyer and a ridiculous witness, he was sent to jail for the rest of his life. To spend his remaining years as a convicted felon. No one would believe him, no one. His appeals, they were a joke. And even though he pleaded, it was always—"You raped her, killed her, pay the piper." Put yourself in his place for one minute. See, they didn't know about DNA back then. Circumstantial evidence! So they let him rot there, twenty-four years. Then, this last trial, the DNA was presented, and it was over in a flash. Proof was always right there. But what about him, huh, his life, his family? The twenty-four years that he wasn't there! I'll never forget the look in his eyes, the sound he made the moment they acquitted him, let him go. And we all ran to him, my mother, my brothers, my sisters, and me. Hugged him so tight, never wanted to let go . . . That's your legal system. And that's what it did to me and my family.

# ALFRED

25 to 40
comedic

*Alfred has come to terms that he's nuts.*

(*Manic.*) Crazy insane thoughts. Nuts, nuts! So finally one day I came to the conclusion—I'm out of my mind! And you know how good it felt to finally accept, admit that I'm CRAZY! You know how liberating that feels? I mean all those years of trying to pretend I was sane, normal. But then one day to finally admit to myself I AM STARK RAVING MAD, A LUNATIC! See these eyes, see them? Crazy, huh? These are the eyes, Linda, of a mentally unbalanced man. KOO-KOO! KOO-KOO! (*Beat, a little softer.*) And well, I was wondering about you. See, I saw something, something in your eyes. Water seeks it's own, you know. You're like me, I can feel it. Tell me Linda, are you, are you nuts too? (*A beat.*) Look, I know this must seem like lot for a first date. But you just said, "Tell me about yourself." And well, why beat around the bush? So, are you? Tell me Linda, are you, are you a lunatic, too?

# JOE KLIEN

40s to 50s
comedic

*A dead man who decides to become
an actor.*

The day I died I couldn't figure out where I wanted to go, y'know? See, when you're dead you can do anything, go anywhere. Most people don't know that. I mean you don't find that out 'til you die. Like most guys I believed there was this heaven-hell thing. Well take it from me, it doesn't exist. Anyway, I died and had to make some decisions here. When I was alive, I was a cop, twenty-two years. That's how I got shot, botched drug bust. Anyway, I always loved going to a good movie. Wondered about the actors, acting. They get so much money y'know, for just making believe. Cops, fireman, we make near to nothing. Heard Harrison Ford gets like twenty million a movie. That's a lot of money! So I have decided in death to come back and become an actor. S'never too late, right? And I hear you have to go to these monologue auditions here to get acting jobs, s'why I'm here. Gonna do a monologue for you in a minute, a minute monologue. But first let me ask, does Harrison Ford really get twenty mil a movie? I mean does he make that much?

# JOHNNY

seriocomedic
20s to 30s

*A drunk, bitter man attending
a family wedding.*

*(Somewhat drunk.)* I don't know, man. I look at them
and wonder, am I in the right family? Maybe I was accidentally switched at birth. I mean, I'll try talking to Aunt
Helen or whoever, and after maybe a minute or two,
there's nothing left to say. All this dead air. So I'll go have
me a drink or two. And when I get a nice buzz going, I'll
go back to Aunt Helen or whoever, give it another shot,
try talking to her. And I'll feel like I'm really *getting her*.
I'll be into this heavy rap about some relative or something, when I notice she's looking at me with *disdain*. Her
disgust, disapproval, I can feel it. And it really pisses me
off! She just can't bear to see me happy, a little buzzed.
So I just walk away, yeah, leave her there, screw her! At
least, at least I made the attempt! At least I tried! *(Getting
louder, angrier.)* See, I couldn't care less about her or any
of them! I just see them at these stupid weddings or . . . !
*(Then.)* Hey, where you going? I was talking to you.
What happened? Where you going?!

# HOWIE
20s to 30s
dramatic

*Howie lambastes his father for being rude to
an attendant.*

Does that make you feel strong, Dad, huh? Important?
How could you? That poor guy takes pride in what he
does. It may not be much, but to him, to him it's everything! So maybe he didn't go to college, or even high
school, but what he does here . . . He's got his dignity,
Dad, and you just tried to take it away from him. The way
you talked to him just now, like he was nothing. Maybe
handing out towels in a men's room isn't as prestigious as
being a big CEO, but . . . You know, y'know, let's forget
dinner, Dad. Suddenly, suddenly I lost my appetite.

# GREG

20s to early 30s

seriocomedic

*A tourist in New York City for the first time.*

*(Very excited.)* You walk out an elevator, say hello, and next thing you know, well here we are! Here you are! God, I love New York! This could never happen where I'm from. Mean there's like two thousand people in my whole town. You are so beautiful, you are. You're probably the most beautiful . . . ! And being here with you now, my God, this was, this was . . . incredible! God, I love New York! Just got here this week. I'm sure you can tell, huh? Tourist, right? Written all over me? Anyway, I've seen just about everything, museums, galleries, plays. Been going almost twenty-four/seven since I got here. And today, meeting you, and then one two three, here, my hotel room. And you were amazing! This was the most . . . *(Heartfelt.)* You are an incredible woman, you know that? Inside and out, incredible! *(A beat, taking out his wallet.)* *Now*, how much did you say? Two hundred, right? Two hundred dollars? *(Handing her money, heartfelt.)* Thank you, thank you so much; I really mean it. *(Then, with delight.)* God, I love New York!

# REG

20s to early 30s
comedic

*Reg, a soap opera star, talks of an embarrassing experience he had in a health club.*

I was at the hotel health club, running on the treadmill. Folks were staring at me. People talking, pointing. Happens all the time. I'm a daytime soap star, comes with the territory. So I tried to focus on the TV, changed a channel or two, pretend I don't notice them. I mean, sometimes soap fans can be, well, invasive. See, when you're a soap star, no matter where you go, people always recognize you. Happened even there in a health club in Pit Stop, Idaho, where I was doing some publicity for the show. Then I noticed more people stopping, pointing. Finally I decide, what the hell, I'll sign some autographs. But then the guy on the next treadmill taps me on the shoulder, says, "Mister, every time you flick the goddamn remote you're changing all the TVs here, we can't watch our own shows! "Oh," I say, "I'm so sorry." I put down my remote. Everyone turns back, grumbles, and starts running on their treadmills again. After a minute or two, I stopped, slithered into to the locker room, got dressed, and left. What a lesson in humility that was.

# WILIFRED

40s to 50s

seriocomedic

*A man gives a stern lecture to a young boy about pollution.*

And old Mother Earth she gets mad, I mean real pissed. Gets sick and tired of all the shit man has heaped on her. The pollution, filth, total disrespect. Mother Earth feels raped; so she decides to have her revenge. So one day, when man least expects it, when he's driving to work or walking his dog, Mother Earth winks and has her way! It's the end of the world, spelled out on her terms. She starts to pop, fizzle, and explode! Sparks fly, fires start, earthquakes. Then volcanoes, tidal waves! Mother Earth is spewing her bile on everything! There's calamity, hysteria— REVENGE! *(A beat.)* And it all began with a little asshole like you. With that piece of paper you dropped on the street just now. And then you just walked away, couldn't care less. You just shit on Mother Earth! Now go pick up that paper, understand?! Or old Mother Earth . . . ! You pick up that paper NOW before she lays havoc on all of us. DO YOU HEAR ME?!

# HARRIS

30s to 50s
dramatic

*Harris recalls seeing a man have a heart attack while he was about to have lunch.*

I was hungry, eager to eat my pastrami sandwich. It was lunch hour, crowded. So I'm sipping my coffee, looking out the window, waiting for my sandwich, when I hear a woman scream. Everyone in the restaurant turned toward her. Across the room a man was holding his chest, his face beet red. "Heart attack!" I heard someone say. Several people rushed over. Next thing, the guy's on the floor, people leaning over him. "Call 911!" Cell phones were out, people calling. And we all stood there, waiting, quiet. Is he dead? Did he die? Ambulance arrived within minutes. Then a buzz went through the restaurant, "He's okay!" And everyone sits down again, goes back to their meals. They rolled him out through the rear entrance. Passed right by me, oxygen mask on his face. And I don't know why but I waved to him, this stranger, as he left. He smiled, gave me a big thumbs-up. I sat down and there was my pastrami sandwich, waiting for me. I took a bite, then another. Tell ya, was the most delicious pastrami sandwich I ever had.

# MARK

20s to 40s

comedic

*Mark is upset about being interrupted while trying to write.*

What? What do you want? Can't you see I'm busy? I'm writing! God, you piss me off! You do this all the time, you do. It's like you just wait for me to build up my momentum. Just when I get things going, when I have an idea that's . . . Don't look at me like that! That won't work! That will not work! I'm writing here, busy! You have to wait! *(He looks away and then back, slowly caving in.)* You hate the snow, it's snowing out! *(Giving up.)* Shit. Get your leash. Go ahead. Get your leash! I'm warning you, you better go as soon as we get out there. I don't want to be standing . . . *(Softening.)* All right. All right. *(Smiling.)* All right. You win.

# JOHN DICKSON FISHER

40s to 50s
dramatic

*John talks of his cancer scare.*

When he came in, he said, "We just don't know, need to take more tests." But there was a look in his eyes, he knew. He was lying. He was standing there with the other doctors, all of them looking at me like I just peed my pants or something. It felt like there was this long corridor between me and them. Like they were miles away. No one wanted to say it, that it could be, that it was—cancer. They're professionals, better than any poker players, but their eyes, their eyes were giving it away. So you slowly sink into your seat. You want to cry, but you can't. You want them to hold you, but they can't. So you sink deeper until you succumb. And then, you accept. *(A beat.)* A few days later he called. His voice seemed so guarded. And then he finally told me. You have no idea what that moment feels like. I simply said, "Okay, thank you." And he repeated it, "You're fine, fine. We didn't find a thing. You're not going to die." Did he say that, did I—or did I just think it? And I breathe, breathe, and say, "Thank you. Thank you." And I hang up. And I say it again and again, "Thank you. Thank you."

# GABE

20s to 30s
comedic

*Gabe confesses to a fellow worker that he's
really a fairy.*

I'm a fairy. Now you know. So is Nate. We both are. I
had to tell you. People in the office are starting to talk. I
know. I hear. I've heard. And I didn't want you to get
your hopes up, you're very nice. See, Nate and me, well,
we're not the only ones. Truth be told, a lot of people
here at Pillsbury are fairies. Every department, every division—we're everywhere. See, we thought Pillsbury would
be the ideal company to operate from. You know, Pillsbury, *angel* food cake. Never thought anyone would catch
on. Dumb thinking, huh? Angels, fairies, it's a whole different thing. *(A beat.)* Well, now you know. So if you notice anyone being exceedingly nice, be aware, they're
probably fairies too. Our kindness, they say, it's a dead
give away. Fairies just can't help being nice. Now if you
don't mind, I'm going to take my shirt off and *finally* let
my wings out. *(He starts to open his buttons.)* I hate hiding, being so secretive. *(Smiling.)* I'm tired of being a *clos-
eted* fairy. Wait, just wait'll you see my wings.

# LEONARD
50s to 60s
dramatic

*Leonard talks about realizing his mother
has Alzheimer's.*

The first time I noticed was on the phone, our weekly conversation. Her voice seemed a little different. Then the phone calls, they got weirder. At first I thought, okay, she's just getting older. But when I came down here to visit, that's when I saw it. I mean my mother was so beautiful, always took such good care of herself. Now she doesn't even comb her hair. She just sits there and . . . You pretend not to notice, you know. Try to keep the conversation going. But you realize she's changed, different. Everything is. *(A beat.)* It's up to me, isn't it? I have to make the decision here, don't I? She can fall, hurt herself. I'm sure you've heard this all before, haven't you? This is the right thing I'm doing, isn't it? . . . She'll be happy here, won't she? Won't she?

# SEAN

Late teens
comedic

*Sean reveals his dream to be a rock star.*

I'm gonna be a rock star, man! And everyone's gonna know my name, everyone! And I'm gonna get laid a lot, cause rock stars have orgies and everything! Asians, black girls, even Jewish chicks, man. Be beggin' for me, every night, at my hotel door. 'Cause rock stars are royalty! And I'm gonna be badder than the Stones and bigger than the Beatles! And rock stars get lots of drugs, man, designer drugs. People just give 'em to you. And I will snort endless amounts of everything, be buzzed all the time. Until finally, in some stadium somewhere, I will OD, in front of thousands of adoring fans. Drama, flashbulbs, pandemonium! And it'll be in the papers and on TV. And they'll have to take me to rehab. I'll get like a million fan letters. Then I'll have a miraculous COMEBACK! Get to play bigger stadiums, get movie offers, books, everything! *(A beat.)* And all I gotta do is just get out of here. Get out of this hell-hole town. So I need you to advance me the money, man. I'm good for it, pay you back. I promise man, I swear. I swear, man.

# CHRISTIAN
20s to 30s
comedic

*Christian freaks out when he learns
he has only one minute to do a
monologue for an audition.*

One?! One minute?! You're kidding. What can you . . . ?
ONE MINUTE?! By the time I say, "Hello, my name is . . .
My monologue's from . . ." One minute's not enough! I'm
an actor. I've worked hard, studied for years. Can't you
give me at least two, c'mon, two minutes, please? Two
minutes!—All right, all right, how about a minute and a
half. Minute and a half, that's just a half minute more! A
half a minute! Look, I know you're busy, got a lot of actors to see. I totally respect your time, but one minute is
just . . . It's *disrespectful!* I am an actor. I . . . *(Stops.)*
What? My time's up? But I didn't do . . . I haven't done
my monologue yet. *(Then, softly, sadly, as he leaves.)*
Sure. Sorry. Thank you.

# MARSHALL
## 30s to 40s
### dramatic

*Marshall, a prisoner on death row,
tries to convince his lawyer not to go
for any more appeals.*

It's not like I saw bright lights or angels singing. It's more like a shift, change of mind, different point of view. See, I've come to totally accept that what I did was wrong, terrible. And those families, they deserve better. I killed six women, man. Cold blood. Their families deserve . . . I NEED TO DIE NOW! No more appeals, all right? Stop the prolonging. I want you to go in there and tell 'em it's over—endgame. And I'm going to go back to my cell and pray for everyone, everywhere. You did a good job. You're a good lawyer, but it is time to cut our loses. Go ahead. Go tell them it's over. Let them sleep well tonight. Be a good guy, go.

# TAD

30s to 40s

seriocomedic

*Tad reveals to his wife that he secretly had a brother who was a criminal.*

There's something I have to tell you . . . I have a brother. Well I *had* a brother, he's dead, died a couple of days ago. They found his body in a dumpster near a motel, few miles from here. They don't know how he died, but they say he was brutally murdered. I know I should have told you about him, but he was kind of the black sheep of the family. Y'know, drugs, jail. Haven't seem him in years. Well, he called here a few days ago. You were at your mother's. Asked me to meet him at this motel. Figured he needed some money so I said no. But he pleaded, so I went. He looked terrible. I'd never seen him look so bad—dirty clothes, filthy. And from the minute I got there, we did nothing but argue. Soon we went from arguing to fighting. Lamps broke, the room was wrecked. But when I left, when I left that motel, he was alive! Bloody, beaten, but alive. And now, now the cops think I did it. I swear, I SWEAR, I didn't! When I left he was . . . I know I should have told you, I know. But you have to believe me about this, you have to.

# RALPH

20s (in human years)
seriocomedic

*Ralph is aching to be adopted.*

What, what are you looking at? Why you staring? What, you want to know something about me, some *background information*? Don't you have anything better to do than just stand there and judge me? I go through this all day. Make up your mind! *(A beat.)* Hey, you want me to look cute for you, that what you want, cute? Well, let me tell ya, I do cute very well. *(He makes a cute face.)* I do cute better than anyone, anyone here! Want me to roll on my back, huh? *(He looks lovingly.)* How's that, you like that? SO MAKE UP YOUR MIND! You have any idea how many times a day I go through this every day? It's exhausting! How can you resist me? I'm housebroken for Christ's sakes! C'mon, c'mon, take me home. I'm great with kids, can fetch on cue. All right, all right, I'm no puppy, who is? That puppy crap's overrated. I got experience, learned life lessons— Hey, hey, where you going? Where you going?! You want cute? I can . . . ! I can roll over, retrieve! *(A beat, bitterly.)* Hope you get a puppy with worms. This torn newspaper here is just fine. This cage here is perfect. Who needs you? WHO NEEDS YOU?!

# SAM
40s to 50s
dramatic

*Sam recalls a tender moment
with his mother.*

It was a moment, just a moment, that's all. We were outside the restaurant, had just finished dinner. The valet was getting our car. I was standing behind her. Maybe I had too much to drink, I don't know. But for some reason I placed my hand on her shoulder. Unusual. I don't usually . . . She was sitting there in the wheelchair, looking straight ahead, kind of spaced out. Then she did something that genuinely surprised me. She placed her hand on mine, and she left it there. She didn't look up or smile . . . She just touched my hand, started patting it. I can't remember the last time . . . I mean this was a woman not known for her warmth. At first I wanted to pull my hand out from under hers. It was too . . . ! But I left it there. And she continued patting it, as if this moment was so natural. I'll never know if she even knew what she was doing. Maybe it was just the dementia. But it didn't matter. To me, that moment, well, it was wonderful. It was a moment I'd waited for my whole life.

# LUKE

30s

dramatic

*Luke tells how a young criminal
almost killed him.*

She just showed up, my cabin in the country. Had no idea
who she was, or even how she found my place. I mean
I'm in the middle of the woods. But there she was standing at my door. Said she was lost, could I help her. I felt a
bit like the wolf in Little Red Riding Hood. Maybe it was
the way she looked at me, so innocent. But . . . there was
this playful look in her eyes too. It was then I began to
wonder, hey, who's the wolf here? Told her I didn't have a
phone, left my cell at home. She said it didn't matter,
could she please come in, it was so cold. She was maybe
seventeen. But from the moment she sat down, I knew I
was in trouble. I made coffee, told her I'd take her into
town. She started telling me about her life. Abuse, drugs,
running away. And as she talked, she kept moving closer,
closer. And for a moment I thought, hey, why not, who'd
know? But then I said, "I think we'd better go." She
looked at me and said, "No." Her mood changed, suddenly. That's when out she pulled out the knife. Then she
made me get undressed, tied me to the chair, naked. She
became a whole different person. Mean, cold, hard. Told
me I shouldn't mess with minors. What? She started
sweating. Then she took my wallet, my car keys, and left.
Left, just like that. Left me there naked in the chair. Next
thing I smelled smoke. My cabin was on fire! . . . I don't
know how I got out of there. I rolled, tumbled, broke
nearly every bone in my left leg. Burns on nearly a fifth of
my body. Luckily, someone heard me screaming in the
woods. Very lucky . . . Well, the cabin burnt down. Oh,
they found her, yeah, about a month later. Car crash, my
car, dead. Her blood was filled with meth amphetamine.
Sad. Crazy. Crazy.

# IAN

20s to 30s
comedic

*Ian just can't say that scary word "love."*

No, no it's not you. It's just . . . it's the word, okay? I can't say it to anyone. Always. Even my mother. I'll be on the phone with her, y'know, and at the end, she always says, well, y'know, the word. Always. Hate it. It feels like a trap to get me to say it back. But I always just say "Yeah, bye." And you mean a lot more to me than her. So it's not . . . I just can't say it. I've tried. My tongue sticks to the top of my mouth. *(He tries.)* Lo . . . Lo . . . I'm sorry. And if our relationship is *contingent* on my having to say it, then, well . . . You know how much I care for you. What's a word? Long as you allow me this one little thing. To never have to say it. Not in person, not on the phone, not even on a Christmas card. So that's all I have to say on the subject. Let's just go to bed. What time you have to get up? I'll set . . . Hey, where you going? Why you getting dressed? —Hey, what's wrong?

# JACK

30s to 40s

dramatic

*A sergeant confronts a traitor*
*in his company.*

Those were my men, Mike. I trusted you! How could you—how could you do this? Don't you know they'll kill you when they're through with you? You think those assholes are your friends? *(A beat.)* What's it like, huh? What's it like to wake up every morning, knowing you're a Judas?! That you'd cut the throats of guys who'd protect your ass? What's it feel like, huh? *(A beat.)* Two of my men are dead. They're dead because of you! Now two American families have to be told that their fathers, their husbands, are gone because some asshole decided to switch allegiance midstream. You best start praying to your Allah or whoever the fuck you pray to. 'Cause you're going to need all the help you can get, man. I hope they fry you, I do. I hope they burn your ass.

# MIKE
20s to 30s
dramatic

*Mike yearns for love but
pretends he's just working out*

*(An inner monologue.)*
I'm the guy, yeah.

You always see me in the gym, yes.
Every day.
Always focused,

looking straight ahead.
Working out.
Staring in the mirror—at myself.
Focused.
And you think,

must think,

he's so conceited.
But I see you from the corner of my eye.
I do,

yes.
But I never say hello, no.
Never even look your way.
Just stay *focused*
Focused on me, in the mirror.
Pumping, pumping.
But actually
I'm aware,

very aware,

you're there.

And I wish
                    I could stop,
          turn to you,
                    say—"Hello."
Then hold you in my arms
          and kiss you.
                    And make love to you.
I wish.
          I wish.
                    Wish I wasn't
                    so terrified!
That's why I hide here,
                    every day.
Always staring in the mirror
                    at myself.
Watching my muscles grow.
                    As I pump,
and pump,
and pump!

# MICHAEL

20s to 30s

dramatic

*Michael confronts the man
who abused him as a child.*

How's the family, huh? Kids must be in college by now. Sorry I haven't been in touch, but, well, you know. You want know the biggest secret I ever had? Think you might know it. I've kept it in a cupboard in my head. Hidden. All these years. But I'd open that cupboard every once in a while. When I'd try getting serious with someone, POP, there it was, my secret! S'funny how the past can come back and bite you! Like when I'm try to get close to someone, POP, *your* face suddenly appears. Isn't that odd? A wedge, a reminder! Uncle Bob. Wanna know something? I liked it. I liked it when you did it to me back then. Because you were paying attention. Weren't yelling or hitting me like . . . But Uncle Bob, you were the adult, you should have known better. Anyway, that cupboard's wide open now. Know why? I know there were others. You've been busy with the boys, Bobby. We've started a little club, called it The Survivors of Uncle Bob Club . . . So, let's talk business. Let's talk cash or I call the cops . . . You were always my favorite uncle, you know that? Always. Always, Uncle Bob.

# STEPHEN
20s to 30s
comedic

*Stephen tries to talk his way out of
an indiscretion he committed.*

What's this about? Talk, tell me . . . This about last night, that "incident" in the closet? I told you, told you, it was nothing. We were drunk, fell on the floor, that's all. *(Tenderly.)* Honey, c'mon, I love you, you know that. And we are gonna have a great wedding tomorrow. You just have to trust me. I had no idea that guy was gay. To me he was just another guest at the party. We were in that closet looking for a bottle of Absolut, we ran out. And we fell, that's how we ended up on the floor. We used to keep the liquor in that closet, remember? And it's dark in there. So cramped, that's why I was on top of . . . Honey, we have all our guests here from out of town. You just have to pull it together. You'll see, we'll both feel better after brunch. We'll have some nice spinach quiche. Let me fix your hair, c'mon. And we have to do something about that dress before we go downstairs. Let me pin it for you. We are gonna have a great wedding, just wait and see . . . Honey, c'mon, don't look at me like that. Do I look gay?

# DYLAN
30s to 40s
dramatic

*Dylan decides to finally go out in the world.*

It's a beautiful day. I'm going to go outside—soon. Sun's shining, air looks so fresh. Think it's time. I'm tired of sitting here, watching TV. Tired of being inside here for so long. Sitting here in this house, alone. Guess I'm just tired of being tired. Tired of thinking about her all the time. Of mourning for our marriage. It's over, and I'm over it. I'm over her! And now I want to go out! Want to see people, do things. I'm going to turn off this TV soon and leave. That's what I'm gonna do. It's a beautiful day. And I'm gonna go out, I am. I'm going to go outside—soon.

# ROBERT

20s to 30s

comedic

*A neurotic man in a neurotic relationship.*

What, are we competing, huh? 'Cause if we are, you win. You win, okay? If we need to see who's more needy you win, hands down. I didn't just tell you about my family to set up some sort of pity-me rivalry. And you do this a lot, you do. I'll share something sad about myself, and next thing I know, you're telling me how it was worse for you. What is that about? Can't I have a single moment of misery by myself? Must it always be this negative competitive thing? Right now, I just want to be my own tree, okay? Want to stand all alone in my own forest and be miserable. Alone, thirsty, without a drop of rain. I want to become bone dry thirsty. And I DO NOT want any other tree in the forest to tell me how they're more thirsty than me, 'CAUSE I DON'T CARE! To put it another way, if you want to watch my car wreck, you have to promise to just look. You cannot be the other car in the accident! Now I want to continue telling you about my miserable mother. If you feel you must compete, at least let me finish first.

# JOHNATHAN

30s to 50s

comedic

*Johnathan, a singing teacher,
secretly lusts for his young student.*

*(To his student.)* "Let the sound out. Open wide.
From the diaphragm. From the diaphragm! Open. Open."

*(To himself.)* That blouse, that blouse is so revealing.
Luscious. I love your neck. I love your neck! Your skin,
so soft, dark, delicious. And the way that blouse just
barely . . . God, how I'd love to . . . !

*(Speaking to her, the teacher, very professional.)*
"Breathe. Big breath. Full . . . Nice. Continue."

*(Back to inner monologue.)* Come to bed—now! I can
carry you. I can carry you into my bedroom. Then I'll rip
that lovely blouse off, tear those clothes. Lick, kiss every
inch. Make you beg for . . . !

*(Talking to her, very professional.)* "Another breath.
Stand straight. Tall. Much taller. Yes. Correct. Continue."

*(Inner monologue.)* I'll push you down on my bed.
Smell you, lick! Kiss those luscious lips! Then rip my
clothes off. And you'll moan and I'll . . .

*(To her, professional, more urgent.)* "Now finish it.
Hit that note!"

*(Inner monologue.)* Hit it!

*(The teacher.)* "Higher!"

*(Inner monologue.)* Deeper!

*(Teacher.)* "Now breath, breathe!"

*(Inner monologue.)* Lick!

*(Teacher.)* "Breathe!"

*(Inner monologue.)* Sweat!

*(Teacher.)* "Sing!"

*(Inner monologue.)* ECSTASY! ECSTASY!

*(A beat, then, softly, professional, a bit exhausted.)*
"Nice. Very, very nice. That's enough for today. I want you to know I'm very pleased with the work you're doing. You should be very proud of yourself. Your voice is really coming along. Tell your mother I said you're doing excellent work, excellent. Okay, next week, same time."

# MATHEW
20s to30s
dramatic

*Mathew talks about the terror of walking into
a crowded gay bar.*

I hate it when I first walk in. S'like crashing through a glass door. That endless wall of eyes. Everyone undressing you with their cruisy unsaid hellos. I hate it. But when I get to the bar, have a drink or two, well that wall sort of melts. After a couple of vodkas, it all changes. I see smiles, a welcoming committee. Then maybe I'll have another drink, just one more. Party time! Then I get up from my bar stool and float through the crowd, Caesar conquering Rome. Suddenly everyone seems like my new best friend. A smile, a wink. The ocean seems to part, and I'm the new Moses. All those bodies rubbing up against me as I make my way from here to there. No destination in mind, I'm just enjoying the journey. All those men, those *men*! I say a playful hello—but only with my eyes. I smile, I invite, and I wait. And while waiting, well, maybe just one more vodka, or two, tops. As I wait, then lean on the bar. Wait, stand, and smile.

# LYLE

30s to 40s
dramatic

*Lyle shares how his young adopted son
changed his life.*

Thought I had it all figured out. You know, you work hard during the week, and you party hearty on weekends. But eventually it became like a broken record. Got to a point where my life was totally predictable. One night I realized I might never meet anyone, and I realized I was really lonely. Well, I'm not into dogs or cats, and so I thought, why not adopt a child? I've got a good job, I'm responsible. And I love kids. And after some heavy soul searching I realized I wanted a son. So I began the process first thing the next day. The phone calls, the paper work, the interviews. It's not easy, believe me. Being a single guy and . . . And finally, after what seemed like forever, I was on my way to Russia to meet my new son. And from the moment I saw him, from that very moment, I knew. The look in his eyes. Little fingers, little hands. Instant; instantly. On the plane coming back, I couldn't take my eyes off him. It was amazing. *(A beat.)* I call him Charlie. And there's always something to show him, something we can do—always something. And what I love most about him, he's totally—unpredictable.

# CLARK

30s

dramatic

*A husband fed up with his wife's
yelling and whining.*

When I was a kid I was really fat. And sometimes when the other kids made fun of me, or would throw rocks or crap at me, I'd do this weird thing. You see Superman was the hot TV show back then. And I loved watching it. You might say I idolized him, Superman. And so what I'd do when these kids were making fun, throwing stuff, I'd just stand there, yeah. Lock my hands on my hips and stand tall, strong, just like Superman. I could almost imagine my cape flying in the wind. I felt—invincible. And I really didn't feel a thing, nothing. And that's how I feel now, here, with you. Clark Kent has turned into Superman. And your screaming, ranting, see it doesn't really affect me anymore. Want to know why, huh? *(Placing his hands on his hips, Superman style.)* I'm Superman, Superman, baby! So you can yell and scream and all you want. I can no longer hear you. I'm beyond you. I'm—Superman, Superman!

# TED

20s
comedic

*Ted is enraged that his best shoes
have been destroyed.*

I can't believe it. I fell for it. Way you sat there, looking
so . . . What a fool I am, huh? You kind of get a kick out
of this, don't you? Knowing that I'm buying into your act
of innocence. You've pulled this before and every time,
EVERY TIME I fall for it! You'd think by now I'd learn,
huh? Well I'll tell ya, I'm on to you now. And things are
gonna change around here! Don't ignore me. You look at
me! I know you're listening. Don't you dare walk away
from me! *(A beat, softer.)* Listen up missy, from now on, I
will never trust you here alone, ever again. You are *ban-
ished* to the backyard. When I'm not here, you're not
here. And as far as what you've did to my shoes, my
BEST Italian loafers . . . I'm taking it out in dog food.
There'll be less chow in your bowl tonight. Now get out
of my sight, go! Outside, doghouse, now!

# JOSH
30s to 40s
seriocomedic

*Josh talks about a strange dream he had.*

I dreamt I saw a baby in a toilet bowl. It was adorable, an infant, and it was singing. Singing, yeah, right there in the toilet bowl. It was floating on top of the water. And I was standing right next to the baby's mother, who just happened to be my mother also. We were both looking down at this tiny tot in the toilet. And she was so proud, my mother, his mother. And in my dream, I could *feel* her happiness, yeah. And the child began to shake it's tiny little bum. So cute, adorable! And the movement from the baby's tush started stirring the water in the toilet, making like little waves. And before you could say flush, the toilet did. And it flushed the baby down into the abyss below. We stood there, my mother and me, shocked. The baby was gone. And in her hysteria, my mother blamed me. She felt that I had flushed the toilet. Blame, blame. I told her, "No, I didn't!" And finally she believed me. And we both stood there, looking down into the empty toilet feeling this tremendous sense of loss. That happy, singing baby was flushed away forever. And when I woke up, I felt so sad. So very, very sad.

# BILLY

30s to 40s

dramatic

*Billy, a criminal, tells his lawyer that*
*he wants to toss in the towel.*

Are you kidding? You kidding me?! Who asked you, who asked you to, huh? Haven't you got any god-damned compassion?! That girls' parents need some closure, and so do I. I'm tired of all your legal showmanship. I DO NOT want any more appeals, understand?! See, this isn't about me. S'bout you, you greedy little prick. Your picture in the paper, your face on TV, that's what this is really about: your career. Trying to show the world how much you care about me. Yeah, right, sure. I killed those girls, I was convicted, and now it's over. Now go out there and tell 'em Billy-boy is throwing in the towel. Put on your phony caring face and say we had a change of mind. Tell 'em to gas up that chamber; I'm ready. Don't look at me like that. I'm on to you. Now stop being such a goddamned—lawyer—and go tell them no more!

# ROB

20s to 30s

seriocomedic

*Rob tells his wife where he
disappears to all the time.*

*(Very serious.)* I'm going to tell you something. I don't
want to frighten you, okay? Remember that time, just before we got married, you know when we went down to
the Caribbean? Remember how I kept disappearing every
day, and you got worried? And when I got back I told
you I just went for a walk. But you didn't believe me, remember? And that other time a couple of years ago, when
I went on all those business trips, and you were so suspicious. You were convinced I was lying, remember? And
all those other times, when you accused me . . . I'm gonna
tell you the truth. Honey . . . I'm from another planet, a
planet called Zeno. And we've come here to earth to take
over your planet. We need human brain cells. Our civi-
lization is dying and . . . *(Suddenly smiling.)* Honey, I'm
pulling your leg! I was kidding! You're always so suspicious, I figured . . . . You actually believed that?! God! I
just wanted to scare you. *(A beat.)* Well I'm going to
*beam* myself into the bathroom. I'll be right back. *(As he
leaves.)* You actually believed all that? God, you're
gullible.

# MIKEY

30s to 40s
comedic

*A cheating husband
trying to leave his mistress*

C'mon, don't look at me like that. Don't do that, you
know it makes me nuts. I mean wasn't it great just now,
huh, wasn't it? Wasn't that sex we just had INCREDI-
BLE?! Three times in a row, thought I was gonna have a
heart attack here! And it wasn't just the sex. And you
would know, you would, 'cause you're smart. Wasn't just
the sex. No one can pull the wool over your eyes. You're
bright, that's what I like about you. Knew it the first
minute I met you. S'why I hired you. *(A beat.)* Look, I
gotta go, she's waiting. The kids, dinner, I'm late. I swear
if it wasn't for those kids . . . ! I'll see you tomorrow, in
the office . . . Oh yeah, don't forget to bring the key
down to the desk. They get real pissed when you leave it
in the room. *(One last look.)* God, you make me crazy!
*(Smiling.)* There oughta be a law against you!

# JEFFREY
## 20s
### seriocomedic

*Jeffrey is trying to open up
emotionally for an audition.*

*(An inner monologue.)* I am trying. I'm standing here desperately trying to show you my emotions, my feelings, but I can't. I'm trapped; I'm in my head. The words, they're coming out, yeah, but there's nothing underneath, I know. I'm emotionally dead up here. God, this pisses me off! I feel like stopping right now and saying, "I'm better than this, I am! Just a few hours ago, you should have seen, I was all loosey-goosey with feelings at home. I was emotionally FULL! Laughter, tears, I was—connected!" But when I walked in here, introduced myself, it was like this giant gate came crashing down. My mouth suddenly went dry, my arms got heavy. You must be thinking, "Send this one back to acting school." But I am better than this, really! You should have seen my rehearsal at home . . . I'm wonderful—at home. Do you make house calls? I'm really sucking up here. I'm better than this. Really. Really I am. Shit.

# HARRY

50s to 60s

seriocomedic

*A husband fed up with his "New Age" wife.*

I don't know you anymore, Anne. You keep telling me you're "evolving." Well let me tell you, the "work" you've been doing on yourself, I think it's a bunch of crap! And if you use that word "empower" once more . . . ! Where's the lady I used to love? That wonderful woman who gave me kids and would cook and keep house. Where is she?! You've changed all right. Now you're more macho than me! You and your women's groups and your power breakfasts. Maybe I'm old-fashioned, but I liked things the way they were. You were home, we'd watch TV, maybe send out for pizza, Chinese, whatever. What was wrong with that, huh, what? *(A beat.)* I miss who you were. And I don't like who you've become. And if you can't "evolve" your way back to the way it use to be, I'm gonna "empower" myself and leave you, understand? Now take that to your power breakfast and chew on it!

# DR. GERALD ZERENFELD
40s to 50s
comedic

*A doctor fed up with the way
his family treats him.*

*(Frustrated.)* In my office I'm God, understand? My patients look up to me. They worship my every word. I'm admired, respected! But then I come home, and how do you all treat me? I'm either ignored, or looked down on, or laughed at. Laughed at, by my own spoiled daughters. And then I'm debased, humiliated. Humiliated, yes, by you. You, my for-better-or-worse wife. I mean how *dare* you ask me—no, no—*tell me* to go empty the garbage. The *garbage*, me, the guy who is God every day in his office! Who saves lives, whose patients cling . . . ! No, I will not empty the goddamned garbage! Isn't that what we hired a housekeeper for?! *(A beat, composing himself.)* I am going upstairs to my den to read my paper and relax. If you want to see me, to apologize, I'll be upstairs on my throne. *(He scowls, gives a regal wave good-bye, and then as he leaves.)* I am God. God, understand?!

# ARNOLD

late 20s to 40s

seriocomedic

*Timid Arnold shares his violent thoughts.*

I have these imaginary conversations in my head. You know, things I *should* have said. And in my mind-talks, I am the ultimate, end-all alpha male. Say things I'd never have the nerve to say. And in my mind, I love how I look, how I sound, what I say. Love standing up to all those pricks in my office who put me down every day. Those guys who laugh behind my back, never sit with me at lunch. Who make me st . . . st . . . stutter when I talk to them. But in my mind-talks I never stutter, no. I have a calm, powerful Darth Vader voice. And I love the look of shock on their faces when I pull out my gun. See, in my head, I have a pistol in my hand. And I'm holding it right up to my boss's head. Watching him and everyone in the office beg for their lives. Then there's that wonderful moment when I decide to kill them. Last looks. No goodbyes. Then I slowly pull the trigger and BANG, blood splatters on every wall! I feel like God or something! . . . But then the phone rings, and I'm back at my desk. It's someone from accounting yelling at me. So I st . . . st . . . stutter an apology, then hang up, and look out my window. And I think and dream how some day, some day, yeah, some day, soon.

# KEN
20s
seriocomedic

*Ken recalls how glorifying his acting career got him into trouble.*

Things had been really slow, depressing. Hadn't gotten an acting job in so long, was all bummed out. And I bumped into this actor friend of mine. He asked what I was up to. And rather than just whine about how lousy things were, I told him I'd just gotten cast in a large role in a film opposite Johnny Depp. Johnny Depp, yeah. Have no idea why I told him that, I just did. And my friend went, "Wow!" and I went, "Yeah." And for that moment I almost believed it, and it made me feel good. Anyway, a couple of days later, I bumped into another actor friend. Told him I'd just gotten the lead, yeah, the lead in a movie opposite Julia Roberts. Julia Roberts, right! And my friend went, "Wow!" And I went, "Yeah! And for that moment I actually believed it. Went on and on about the audition, and how nice Julia was to me, and I really believed it, believed it all. And it made me feel really good! Well soon I started getting all these phone calls from actor friends, congratulating me about all my good news. And I'd tell each one of them a bigger lie. A film for Steven Spielberg, a lead in a Broadway show, my own TV series: I just kept pouring it out! And they all, all of them, went, "Wow!" and I went, "Yeah! YEAH!" And by now I *totally* believed all of it! And I figured hey, since I'm going to be such a big star, I need a new wardrobe. So I went on a buying spree, Barney's, Hugo Boss, the best. Then I started taking all my friends out to dinners at expensive restaurants. Would sit there, telling them about all my upcoming movies and plays. And everyone went, "Wow! Wow!," and I'd yell, "Yeah! Yeah!! YEAH!!" *(A beat, then softly.)* So that's why I'm here, looking for work. Anything. I am thousands and thousands of dollars in debt. I'm desperate, broke, I'll do anything. Dishwasher, janitor, scrub floors. I lied and lied, and my life's a mess. And all I can think now is *(Softly, sadly.)* "Wow. Yeah. Yes."

# CHARLES

30s to 50s

seriocomedic

*Charles talks about his manic mind.*

My head gets so full! Thoughts, unspoken chatter. Yatta-da, yatta-da. I'm run over by my own thoughts, now isn't that odd? And finally I collapse into a chair in complete despair. YATTA-DA, YATTA-DA! I hold my hands to my head and scream, "Stop, stop!" But it just continues, the yatta-da, yatta-da. Makes me crazy. So finally I just *yank* my head from it's socket! Yeah, rip it out from its roots, right from the neck! And I stand there, holding my detached head in my hands, as it sputters away. Yatta-da, yatta-da. Gently, I place it in the chair next to me. And it continues to splatter and chatter on the chair, until finally, thank God, it stops. Stops, quiet. And there's peace, a lovely calm. And I sit there and see my head, not moving, immobile. Wishing it could always be that way. But unfortunately, no, it can't. And after too brief a respite, I slowly lift it up, place it back in it's socket, until I hear the suction. It reattaches, revs up, reboots. And then once again the endless chatter: yatta-da, yatta-da! Yes, it begins again. As always, another day. Another day, of unspoken chatter—yatta-da, yatta-da—in my head.

# HAROLD
40s to 50s
comic

*Harold, accused of infidelity by his wife, confronts her.*

I'll tell ya, you think you know someone. You live with them, raise a family. Then one day you come home, like today, and out of the blue you, my wife, accuses me of being unfaithful. Let me tell you something, you are a paranoid prisoner of your own mistrust. A victim of your miserable imagination! I have done nothing wrong, nothing! Just because you found a pair of panties under the backseat in my car, you rush to judgment! There's a million reasons those panties could have been there. But the real question here is what were you looking for in the first place, huh? Huh?! And that condom wrapper you found mean's nothing, NOTHING AT ALL! You ever happen to think that maybe someone could have broken into my car while I was working late every night last week. I mean my car was right there in the parking lot. Anyone could have . . . And those escort service cards you found in my wallet, I have no idea where I got them. People hand me cards all day. Real question here is what were you doing in my wallet in the first place, huh? Mistrust. Things aren't always like they seem. Just remember, what may look like water may only be just a mirage.

# PETE

*A son tells his father about his night.*

I was with Barry, Pa. You know my friend with the one leg who drools all the time. Barry, the guy with the glass eye, him. Anyway, we're at Kelly's last night, trying to pick up chicks. I like to hang with Barry 'cause next to him I look really good. Anyway, we're shootin' the shit, when this dude comes in with a gun, a gun, yeah. Says it's a holdup. Bartender immediately gives him all the money in the register. And Barry says something like, "Holy hit!" This crook hears him, puts the gun up to Barry's head, and says, "You a wise guy?" Barry just stands there, sweating, slobbering, scared. I turn to the crook and say, "Can't you see he's sick?" Well, I guess he felt sorry for him, you know, 'cause of Barry hardly having any teeth, and that terrible skin. He took Barry outside. And then a few minutes later Barry came limping back in. We left, just as the police arrived. I asked Barry what happened. And he took out over five hundred bucks. Was a gift from the crook, like a Robin Hood thing. So me and Barry went over to McDonald's and had like a big party, yeah. Hanging out with him is so cool.

# PAUL

30s to 40s

seriocomedic

*Paul recalls how his love to paint*
*nearly killed him.*

Paint, just paint, that's all. That's all I ever wanted to do.
And when mother died, I finally could. Paint, full time. So
I started that very morning, right after the funeral. Went
out and bought hundreds of canvasses and paint supplies.
I started, I began. God, how I loved the smell of the
paints, loved the colors. The pinks, yellows, blues. Started
making all kinds of strokes with my brush. First wide,
then small. I'd jump up and down and cover a whole canvas! Wild, abstract designs. For the first time in my life I
was expressing myself! I'd cover a canvas, then immediately start another. Rainbows, rivers, anything. I couldn't
care less about meals, social engagements. I wanted, no,
NEEDED to express myself! Browns, oranges, reds! Fill
another canvas, then another! Time was melting. Clouds
and winds of color were flying across my canvasses. The
phone would ring, I wouldn't answer. The doorbell, I'd
ignore it. I was painting, painting from my soul! One canvas after another! The paint started spilling all over me, it
felt wonderful! Then I . . . I started rolling around in it,
yeah, the paint. The colors covering me. Grays, blues,
browns! Soon I became my own canvas. The paint fell on
my face, spilled in my ears. I started rolling around in it! It
got it in my mouth, my eyes! I couldn't see, no, but I could
*feel* the colors, *feel them*! Then I started swallowing it, the
paint. Drinking, pouring can after can, can after . . . ! *(He
stops, then slowly.)* I don't remember, have no recollection

how I ended up here. Perhaps my housekeeper, Janet, maybe she found me, called the . . . They told me I'm lucky I'm alive. Lucky I'm not blind. Lucky I used watercolors . . . Mother's death, maybe it was more than I could . . . I just wanted to paint, that's all. Express myself. Paint.

# WOMEN'S MONOLOGUES

# JULIANNE
30s to 50s
seriocomedic

*In an inner monologue, Julianne,
a bitter, unhappy wife, reveals
her secret thoughts as she watches
her husband eating his breakfast.*

I hate feeling, no, KNOWING you're judging me. You are, you know you are. But my darling, I have learned to live with it. I've come to realize it's the only way you can feel *superior*. So go ahead, immerse yourself in your stupid opinions. I have learned to make myself feel invisible. Invisible. Your stares don't matter any more. So sit there, sip your coffee, and smile. That stupid *smirk* tells me you're judging me. And then you'll go back to reading your paper. And then I'll say, *(Gently, polite.)* "More coffee, darling?" And you'll nod that superior, condescending nod, as I pour and you watch me from the corner of your eye. As I take little bites of my toast. Tiny little bites . . . But next time, next time, when I pour you your coffee . . . *(Feigning upset.)* "Oh my darling, I'm so sorry! It was an accident; accident!" The scalding hot coffee, burning your eyes. "I'm so sorry!" Terrible. *(Smiling.)* And you'll be blind. Blind. —But eyes that can't see, can't judge. — Maybe I'll do that. Yes. Maybe I will. Maybe.

# SHARON

late teens
dramatic

*A girl who may have met
the right guy at a party.*

I just needed to get away from all that noise, you know?
It's so crowded in there. I like to come out here by the
lake sometimes, look up at the stars. So calm, quiet. *(A
beat.)* Y'know, sometimes I feel like I'm from another
planet, isn't that crazy? Like I just somehow ended up
here on earth. That I'm like a whole different species.
And I don't understand the people here. I mean, I look at
them in there, watch their mouths move, hear their
words, but I have no idea what any of them are saying,
what they mean. Isn't that weird? . . . I saw you standing
there in the corner, and there was just, I don't know,
something in your eyes. Way you were just staring up at
the ceiling. Way you were leaning on that wall, like you
were trying to hold it up or something. And when I came
over, said hello, the way you stared at me like you knew
me, or wanted too. I kinda feel like we do know each
other, y'know, sort of. Isn't that crazy? . . . You don't
have to say anything. We can just sit here, look up at the
sky . . . I like when it's quiet like this. *(A beat, looking
up.)* It's such a nice night, isn't it?

# ELIZABETH
20s to 30s
seriocomedic

*Elizabeth recalls the last time
she saw her boss.*

You arrogant bastard, no wonder no one likes you! That's
what I should have said. But I didn't, I just thought it.
You don't say things like that to him, not him, no. Not
unless you want to be fired. But I was this close, this
close! He told me I had to work again all weekend. Even
though I'd just told him, I had plans, family. But he just
sneered, said he was sorry, he needed me. So I stormed
out of there. Said, "Fine, sure, okay!" Sat at my desk and
fumed. I was furious! And so I was just about to call you,
to cancel, when I heard like a crash, then a moan. I got
up, went to his door, knocked. Nothing. Then I heard another moan, went inside, saw him lying there on the floor.
He looked terrible, Terry. Pale, pasty. I bent down, didn't
know what to say. He seemed so frightened, fragile. He
tried to touch my face with his hand. It was like a really
tender moment. And then I held him. And then—then he
died, yeah, right there in my arms. I was the last person
he ever saw. Me, who he always humiliated, tormented,
tortured. There he was, Terry, dead in my arms. And he
looked so pathetic. Then I got up, went over and sat in
his chair, his big, brown chair. Looked around his office.
Y'know, I never noticed, but he has a very nice office.
Spacious, nice. And you know what I started to think
about? Unemployment; unemployment, Terry. I wondered, if your boss dies in your arms, are you eligible?
Then I wondered how much I'd get every week. And

then, well, then I called the police. And while waiting, I slowly began to swirl around in his chair. Just swirl around, watching the room go by. I just sat there, Terry, in his big, comfortable brown chair, smiling, happy, and swirling!

# KATE

30s to 50s

dramatic

*Even though many doctors have said
that Karen's son is brain dead,
here she explains why they're wrong.*

He winked. I saw him. I saw him wink, you understand? Just like he used to. Like he did a thousand times when he was a little boy. I was sitting there, talking, just making small talk. Sitting at his hospital bed, chatting. Talking about everything, nothing. And then I said, "Tommy, you remember those summers up in Monroe, huh? How you loved to swim? How you always wanted to be a lifeguard and save people?" And suddenly he clenched my hand. Clenched it, just like this! And that's when it happened, when he winked. Winked to me, like he'd done a thousand times before. Before the accident. HE WINKED! Don't you see, he was trying to tell me, to communicate, understand? He was trying to say "I'm still here, Mom. DON'T GIVE UP ON ME, MA! DON'T! DON'T!" *(Softly.)* . . . So you can't do it, understand? You can't kill him. It would be murder. He's alive inside. He told me. He winked. I swear.

# PAM

30s to 40s
dramatic

*Pam tells how she ended up waitressing.*

Too much. Too soon. I married too young. And one day it just sort of crashed in on me. Hank, my husband, was at work. Kids were outside, playing, screaming. It was hot, and the air conditioner was broke. I was in the living room, vacuuming, cleaning, sweating. And then, I'll never know why, I turned off that vacuum cleaner. Just stood there in the living room and looked around and listened— to my life. And it was—*overwhelming*! I tried to scream, but nothing came out. The walls felt like they were falling in on me. I ran upstairs, got some money, put it in my bag, and left. Yeah, just like that. Left with the clothes on my back, and the sound of the kids still screaming in the backyard. No good-byes, no regrets, NOTHING! Got on the first Greyhound bus out of there to anywhere. Eventually, I ended up here, this job, this bar, on this island. Where I serve cocktails and tell tourists like you the best places to shop. And I love it, I do. I really love my life here . . . Well, you asked. That's my story. So . . . how about another drink, huh? S'happy hour, two for one.

# YVONNE

50s to 60s

comedic

*Yvonne, a "mature" actress,
defends her choice to host a reality
TV show to her agent.*

There is nothing wrong with it, Jack. I'm fine about it, really. Fact is, let's face it, I'm a "maturing" actress. I'm not going to get those plush roles anymore. But I'll be damned if you'll catch me playing some young twit's grandmother. So this job, being host on a reality TV show, it has a certain "cachet." Sure, it won't win me any more Oscars. But it's a job, Jack, a paycheck. And even I have to pay bills. Houses in Santa Monica aren't cheap, you know. And maybe, maybe this will show those "toddlers" over at Miramax that Momma hasn't been put out to pasture yet. Call them. Call them, Jack, tell them we're interested. Lesbian dwarfs sounds interesting. I think we can make something of this, Jack, I really do. People will be able to relate. I mean if even little *midgets* can fall in love . . . ! *Lesbian Dwarfs, A Love Challenge*. I like it, I like it, Jack. It's smart, clever, interesting. As long as they handle it with class. Call them, make a deal, tell them I'm in.

# SALLY
30s
dramatic

*Sally has just found out some disturbing news about her neighbor.*

I'd be getting my paper, he'd be leaving, going to work. I'd say "Good morning Mr. Gurdcheff. How are you today?" He'd smile, small talk, a nice neighbor, you know? Then I'd get the kids ready for school, and I'd go to work. Just another day. But then that night last week. I was home making dinner, TV's on, the news, when I see him from the corner of my eye, Mr. Gurdcheff, on TV. And they're asking him, "Why'd you kill those kids?" Kill? Kids? Some as young as five. Murdered? Must be some sort of mistake. I began to worry, hey, where are the kids? Why aren't they home from school yet?! I started calling their friends, got frantic, began to panic! But then they walked in, wearing their baseball caps. I hugged them, held them. Then we all sit down for dinner, watched the news. Thirteen children murdered, ages five through twelve. My God, you think you know someone, you know? You see them almost every day. Mr. Gurdcheff, apartment 3B. We'd say hello, small talk, every morning.

# CHARLOTTE
30s to 50s
seriocomedic

*A wealthy wife confronts her husband
about his infidelity.*

It's raining, I'm bored, and you're depressed. So it's the perfect time. We need to talk—about ending this. I'm tired of treading water. *(A beat.)* I know about apartment 7C at the Carlyle. Known for quite a while. So I think you know where I'm heading with this. I hired a detective. There are photographs, many. There, right there on the coffee table in the envelope. Duplicates, naturally. He's very photogenic, your young friend. You both look serenely happy. I can certainly see what you see in him. Nice body. *(A beat.)* I'd like . . . well, you know, I'd like a lot of things. But for now I'm just going to go tell Terrisa to make us some tea. When I get back we just should talk, arrange things. I'm sure you'll be fair sweetheart, you always are. Why don't you just browse through those pictures over there while I'm gone. And when I get back you can put a nice offer on the table. And then we can talk . . . Ted, I strongly advise you to be very generous. As they say, a picture is worth . . . a *million* words.

# CLARISSE

30s to 50s
dramatic

*A mother talks of adopting her son.*

There was this moment, I'll never forget. It's hard to explain. This immediate connection. And all I could see, all I could hear was him. And all I knew was he was the one. I was never so sure of anything! He looked up at me and I knew right away. Eventually I brought him home. He's asleep in the bedroom. So what I'm trying to tell you is that my life has totally changed. I don't have the time . . . What you and I had, our late night little *get-togethers*, as much as I enjoyed it, I'm just not into it anymore. It was fun, really, but . . . No more booty calls, Bob. I'm not available. I'm a mom now. I keep mother's hours. And the only one I'll get up for in the middle of the night is him, my son. So I think it's time for you to go find yourself another booty call girl.

# GAIL
50s
dramatic

*A mother-in-law confronts her son-in-law
about the murder of her daughter.*

We loved you like you were our own son. From the first . . .
All those talks, those plans we made. Those nights we all
ate together and laughed, those wonderful weekends. You
seemed so perfect, the perfect son-in-law. I thought I
knew you. If you were so unhappy with her, you could
have told me, you know that. You could have divorced
her, left her! I didn't know there was some disturbed animal living inside you! Some monster that . . . ! HOW
COULD YOU?! She worshiped you, you know that. You
were her life. How—how could you kill her?! And so
brutally. *(A beat, softer.)* I hope you die, hope they kill
you. And I hope you think about what you've done to
her, all of us, every minute for the rest of your life.

# JENNY
## 20s to 40s
### seriocomedic

*Jenny is a clown for terminal children
on the weekends.*

I just do it, red nose and all. In my real life, I'm this serious businesswoman, yeah. But on weekends I'm Polly the Clown. Yellow wig, pink clothes, big red nose. I wear horns, flashing lights—you should see. And I jump up and down and toss confetti. Make like it's a big holiday for them. And they look up and laugh. The kids, they love it. And when I get that laugh out of them, nothing can beat it, it's the best. But when I go home, end of the day, sometimes I just cry. But it's a good cry. A feeling like I've done something worthwhile. And then I'm right back there the next day. Silly Polly strutting her stuff like some crazed Robin Williams on the red carpet. If you only saw the look in their eyes! *(A beat.)* Try it, go ahead. You may feel a little silly at first, but that's the point. I like to start with the nose, the big red nose. Then when you're up to it, put on the wig. I got you an orange one, bright orange. But start with the nose, the nose comes first. But I guess, I guess the most important thing is to just start, just start.

# JANINE

30s to 50s

seriocomedic

*While traveling in Mykonos, Janine ended up in a job in a souvenir shop.*

I just sit here, yeah. Do stock, inventory, anything. ANYTHING to keep myself occupied! When it rains like today, this shop is desolation row. I'll put the radio on, but I don't know what they're *saying. (A little joke.)* It's Greek to me! So I'll just listen to some Greek music, dance around, and fix a pile of T-shirts or something. You are my first customer today. And it's what, nearly five o'-clock? The rain keeps customers away. *(A beat, a confidence.)* I just wanted to get away, that's all, a little vacation. Picked Mykonos 'cause it looked so charming. And then I fell utterly in love with this place. It—put a spell on me. Been here for over six months now. I ran out of money, had to get a work permit, and here I am. *(Building.)* I left everything, everyone I knew back in the U.S.A. I just seem to stay and stay! *(A whisper.)* I can't seem to leave. *(Then, gaining her composure, smiling.)* Can I show you a nice T-shirt or something? We have a great rain sale today. Half price on those "I Love Mykonos" sailor hats. How 'bout it, huh. Can I show you one?

# ROBERTA

20s

dramatic

*Roberta finally meets her father for the first time in her life.*

I don't know what I feel. I know what I should feel. I mean you're my father. Father, Jesus, just saying the word feels so weird. Always thought you were dead. I can't believe I'm actually standing here, that I found you. Why'd she lie, my mother? She said you died, an accident. But when she died last year my grandmother told me you were . . . This was a mistake, my coming here, wasn't it? I'm sorry if I . . . Maybe I should leave, huh? I should leave, shouldn't I? WELL SAY SOMETHING! Open you're mouth, talk to me. Tell me your side . . . *(A beat.)* I'm rambling, I know, I'm rambling. I don't know what to say. So I'm just . . . Why didn't you ever . . . ? I mean for you're whole life, didn't you ever want to . . . ? Weren't you curious . . . ? Didn't you want to know . . . ? Didn't you?

# ESTELLE

60s

dramatic

*Estelle doesn't want to tell her husband the medical news she received.*

Whatiya want? Whatiya want, huh? Can't you see I'm sittin'? I'm sittin' here, leave me alone. Go back to your book. *(A beat.)* Why you lookin' at me like that? Everything's fine, I told you. Now read your paper! *(A beat.)* YOU BELIEVE THIS MAN?! READ YOUR BOOK! *(A beat, softly.)* The doctor said it was nothing. Said I'll live to be a hundred. Just have to take some pills. Pills, that's all. And I have to go for some treatment in the hospital every . . . I don't know, maybe once a week. No big deal. Why don't you go make some coffee, huh? *(A beat.)* All right, all right, they found something. Nothing, really, a little nothing. A lump. A small, nothing, lump. And he checked it and . . . Said they caught it in time. I just gotta take some pills and go for some treatments. Now go make the coffee. Go ahead, let me sit here in peace . . . Did you hear me? Why are you standing there, huh? Go make coffee.

# MAUREEN
### 13 to 18
### seriocomedic

*Maureen's sad because her mother has left
to go to the Pope's funeral.*

Momma's gone. She left, went to see the Pope. He died,
and momma went to Rome, Italy, to be with him.
Momma, she loved the Pope. Was always talking about
him. He came to this town once, yeah, to visit our church
when Momma was just a girl. And he let Momma sit on
his lap, yeah. Momma said that's when she had her
moment of "divine inspiration." Don't know what that
means but Momma says it changed her life forever. Think
that's why Momma makes us all go to church every
Sunday. And why we have to say grace before every meal,
even breakfast. Momma loved the Pope, even more than
Papa I think. Made Papa so jealous. When she'd start
going on about the Pope, Papa would storm out of the
room . . . Momma was cryin' real bad when she left. Said
she didn't know if she'd ever be back. Said she had to do
God's work in Rome now. Then she gave me a big hug
and her rosary beads. Papa said we're to pretend she's
dead. He said we don't have to go to church anymore or
say grace before meals. God how I miss Momma. I hope
she's happy in Rome.

# JOAN

40s to 50s
dramatic

*Joan recalls the day she found out her son
was killed in Iraq.*

It was a feeling. I don't know how I knew, but I did. The kids were down in the den watching TV, I was in the kitchen, making salad for supper. The radio was on, I was half listening. Then the doorbell rang. Figured it was just someone selling something. Kenny yelled up he'd answer it. But then, I don't know why, I stopped doing what I was doing, went downstairs. Kenny was just standing there. The look in his eyes, I'll never forget. I felt a cold sweat, saw the two soldiers standing there next to him. Their eyes, expressionless. And Kenny said, "It's Dad." Just two words, "It's Dad." I yelled "Don't say another word!" The room suddenly seemed to spin. The sound of the radio and TV seemed to get louder, much, much louder! Then Kenny said it. Even though I . . . "Dad's dead. Dad's dead, Ma." And then . . . well, nothing. Quiet. Silence. Nothing else.

# FRAN

twenties
seriocomedic

*Fran's friend surprised her by asking her to marry him.*

He got down on his knee, front of everyone. There were thousands of people there. Bent down and looked up at me. He looked like a little puppy dog. I thought he was just fooling around, just kidding. But then suddenly it seemed like every one in that stadium was staring at us. And I looked up and saw the two of us up on that big TV screen. I looked at him on his knee, and there were these little tears in his eyes, little puppy-dog tears. Then Fred said, "Fran will you marry me?" It got so silent in that stadium. Then Fred held out the ring and said it again, "Fran, will you marry me?" I mean, didn't he know? Did he think that Jerry and I were just friends? Didn't he know I . . . ? He saw the look in my eyes, and he started to sweat, I mean *really* sweat. And then, well I just got up and ran. RAN through that crowd. Hundreds of people started booing at me, yelling, calling me names. I ran all the way home to be with Jerry. Told him what happened, cried in his arms. Fred was just a friend . . . Jerry and me, we got married about a year later. And Fred, even though we invited him, he didn't come to our wedding.

# JENNIFER

20s to 30s

comedic

*Jennifer recalls meeting a handsome guy
in a bar.*

He was so cute, a real hottie. Had the muscles, looks, everything. And when he said hello, I went down for the count. He had something no one else in that bar had, charisma, personality, whatever you want to call it. I'd gone in there with my friend Mike. We'd been on the beach all day, just stopped off for a cocktail. And Mike invited him over to join us. He said his name was Gary. God he was gorgeous. Well we all stood there, chatting by the pool table. I was just melting, waiting for my moment. We we're all eyes, all of us, looking at each other. Staring, eyes, yeah. But pretty soon I realized Gary's eyes were not on me. Gorgeous Gary was into my friend Mike. And Mike was hooked into him. Can anyone say third wheel? I slowly started to wither and die, right there by the pool table. Rude awakening time. I mean I never knew Mike was gay! Finally, I told them I had to go, but they barely even heard me . . . Well, maybe Mike will tell me all about him tomorrow at work, AFTER he tells me he's gay!

# MARGERIE

20s to 30s
dramatic

*Margerie tells how her postpartum
depression nearly did her in.*

We wanted a baby more than anything. We planned,
hoped, prayed. And when he was born, well I was the
doting mother. Every minute checking to make sure he
was okay. If he'd cry, I'd worry. If he even moved . . . !
But I had these horrible dreams where terrible things happened to him. And I started to worry, was depressed all
the time. Just "the baby blues," they'd say. Give it another day and it'll be okay. But it got worse, much worse.
Got terrible. Then one day they found me walking down
the highway, hysterical, holding my baby. I was certain
someone was trying to hurt him. A car stopped, the people inside asked if I was okay. But I thought they were
kidnappers, so I started running. Soon the police came,
big commotion. They took us to the hospital and . . .
"postpartum depression," that's what they called it. And
once I found out, well, we dealt with it. Pills, therapy—
and time. My son, he's turned out to be a real good kid.
So that's my story . . . Your baby, she's a real beauty. And
I know what you've been going through. Why don't you
tell me about it? Just take your time. Take your time.

# ANA

30s
dramatic

*Ana defends her right to keep her son.*

You can't have him, no. You can't just show up here and DEMAND . . . ! Where have you been all these years, huh?! WHERE?! Me, I went to his crib every time he cried. I fed him, took care . . . You LEFT HIM! *(Softer.)* You *gave him* to us, remember? You kissed him good-bye, and we all agreed, we agreed, it would be final . . . He has a happy life here. Gets everything he wants. Did you see that smile on his face just now? You have any idea what this would do to him, to take him away from us? *(A beat.)* Look, I'm glad you've gotten yourself together. I celebrate your sobriety. But he calls me Mommy now; calls Paul, Dad. We are his parents. So I don't care how many lawyers you have out there. *This* is his home now. *Our* home. And I want you to leave. If you really love him like you say you do, then just leave us all alone, and let us get on with our lives again, please.

# SYBIL

30s to 40s

comedic

*Sybil, a memorial crasher, tells a man she just met why she loves memorials.*

No, I didn't know her. Seemed like a nice person though. Decent. Good. God did I cry. Couldn't help myself. Way people up there were talking about her. She seemed like a saint. I especially liked what the brother had to say. That poor man, crying his heart out like that. S'a real life lesson, you know? Tell them you love them when they're alive, cause after their dead . . . They out of cheese and crackers? Anyway, I'm glad I made this one. Some of these memorials can be such a bore. Snore, snore. I hate to say it, but some people's lives are just not worth my time of day. And I mean that in the kindest way. I try to make at least one or two of these a week. Read about 'em in the obits. I mean you wanna see some real drama, cry some real tears, start comin' to some of these. A person's whole life unfolds right in front of you . . . Well, I'm going to go see if they have any more of those little frankfurter things. Lovely meeting you. Maybe I'll see you again, huh? Remember, just look 'em up in the obits. It's a lovely way to spend a day, and you meet the nicest people.

# GLORIA

20s to 40s

dramatic

*Gloria accidentally burnt down her house.
Here she tries to defend herself.*

I'm not a bad person. I know that's what some people in
this town are saying about me. But it's not true. I'm a
good mother, loving wife. And I love my family. *(A beat.)*
Carl and the kids were asleep. I couldn't sleep, so I was
upstairs in the attic cleaning out some old lamps. Was
about 2 AM I guess. I don't know how that fire started.
They said maybe it was the cleaning fluid I was using,
but . . . All I know is that there was all this smoke and
flames. I panicked, started yelling, "Fire, get out!" Ran
down the stairs, tried to warn Carl and the kids. But with
all that smoke . . . Was terrifying! All I can say is thank
God the fire department got there so soon, and that
everyone's okay. Look, I know how this looks. And yeah,
I know there have been other "incidents," other "acci-
dents," but it's just coincidental. Those other times . . .
I'd never hurt my family. I love my kids and . . . I know
how this looks. But you have to believe me, it was just an
accident.

# ANITA

30s to 50s
dramatic

*Anita finally tells her mother how she feels
about herself.*

Mama, see how pretty I look? Don't I look pretty today?
I've grown up to be a real beauty, huh? Even though you
always told me I never would. Always told me I was too
ugly. You made me feel so bad Mama, you know that?
And I believed you. Thought, well if Mama says so, must
be true. I must be ugly. But look at me now Mama, all
dressed up and pretty. It's independence day! When I
looked in the mirror this morning, seemed like a miracle.
'Cause I liked what I saw. I really liked what I saw in that
mirror, Mama! And I stood there and laughed and cried
at the same time. Know why? 'Cause I finally realized,
you were wrong. All those years. All those things you said
about me. And I realized that you can't call me no names
no more. *(Looking down at her.)* It's independence day,
mama! *(Softly.)* Now you rest in peace. Rest in peace,
mama. I don't think you meant bad. I don't think you
meant to hurt me. I just think you were just unhappy
and—*misinformed.*

# SHELLY

25 to 40

comedic

*Fed up with her boyfriend's overanalyzing everything she says, Shelly finally tells him off.*

Must everything be so damn complicated?! Stop therapy, please! Your therapy is making *me* crazy! S'gotten to the point here where I have to watch every word I say. Worry about you overanalyzing everything! Wringing out meanings I never meant. I'll tell ya something, you were a lot more fun when you were nuts! *(A beat, calming herself.)* Look, what I said, what I said just now, was, "I'm leaving." I'm leaving, no big deal. I'm just going to the grocery store, we're out of milk. I'm not going to South America. I don't have a secret lover. I'm going to the goddamned grocery store, right down the street! Look Larry, I know you have separation and mistrust issues but . . . *(A beat.)* I'm going to the grocery store. I'll be back before you can say "anxiety attack." Now just sit down, relax, and breathe.

# KAMI

late 20s to30s
dramatic

*Kami recalls seeing the man who killed her
sister executed.*

I'm not sure what I thought would happen. But I was
hoping. We all sat there, waited. They brought him in. He
didn't look at any of us. Then they put him on the gur-
ney, strapped him down. Seemed like all of this was hap-
pening in slow motion. I wanted to scream, for him to see
us, our faces. But he just stared up at the ceiling. They
asked him if he had any last words, he said no. I thought,
how could he have nothing to say? You kill eight women
for Christ's sake! Look what you've done to us, our lives!
*(A beat, softly.)* They turned the gas on. He gasped, just a
small . . . And that was it. Just like that. All the trials, the
appeals. And no, there is no closure. That's for movies,
books. I sat there, as everyone started filing out. I sat
there alone and watched as they took him out. I sat and
cried and said her name over and over. "Karen. Karen.
Karen"

# TAMMY

30s to 40s
comedic

*Tammy's boyfriend has left her for
another woman. Here she laments to a friend
how horrible she feels.*

It's not just that he left me, no. It's *who* he left me for.
Have you any idea how humiliating this is? People are
laughing behind my back. It's the *age* thing. She's so
much . . . ! He said he met her at work. That things just
happened. It's the AGE thing that gets me! I mean . . .
she's over eighty! Eighty years old! Did you know that!
Legally blind, a bad heart, and one failing kidney. He left
me for his patient at the nursing home. Tell ya, I want to
go over there right now and yank her respirator right out
of her! *(A beat.)* I'll just wait it out. I mean, how much
longer has she got? Oh the hell with it. C'mon, let's go to
the beach. I need to just lie out in the sun and forget
about it. I don't think I'm going to bother with any
sunblock today. Seems like wrinkles are in.

# KAREN
20s to 30s
dramatic

*Accused of not feeling, Karen defends
herself to her boyfriend.*

No, I do feel. I feel a lot. How can you say that? Just because I don't show my feelings all the time. Just because I
can't cry or laugh at the drop . . . Seems the more I know
a guy, I just get, I don't know, shyer. I know that sounds
weird, but it's what happens. Most girls when they get to
know someone, they open up. I don't know what's wrong
with me. It's not that I'm not feeling any feelings for you,
Frank. I feel a lot! Is any of this making sense? 'Cause
you're looking at me like I'm a lunatic. *(Getting more
desperate.)* Frank, please, put your suitcase down. Stay
Frank, c'mon. See, I'm showing my feelings now. I'm begging. Begging's a feeling, right? I'm begging, Frank, begging! I want you to stay. I'm showing you how I feel. See,
isn't this what you want, to see my feelings Frank? See?
I'm feeling! I'm feeling!

# GRETCHEN
30s to 50s
dramatic

*Gretchen describes the mud slide that almost killed her and her husband.*

We'd been watching TV, bored. Been raining for days. So I said "I'm gonna go out for a walk, Walt." Put on my raincoat, got the umbrella. But when I got outside, I saw all the mud everywhere. Got real scared, ran back in, said, "Walt, come out here!" When he came out, he saw it. The mountain, it was . . . It was like it was moving, sort of oozing. Walt ran back in, grabbed the dog, came running out, said, C'mon, let's go, we're going!" He grabbed my hand and we ran, I mean RAN! We tried to start the car but it was stuck in the mud. So we started running down the mountain, all the way down. I was screaming, dog was barking, was terrible! We kept getting stuck in the mud. It was like a nightmare, like the whole mountain was melting underneath us. But we kept on going, down, down, down! *(A beat, softly.)* Well, we lost everything. Some of our neighbors . . . well. We moved here to the mountain to be safe. To get away from all the danger in the city, all the crime there. Thought this was paradise up here. Safe. Right. Yeah.

# CINDY
late teens
comedy

*Cindy tries to explain why she gave so much money to a telephone fundraiser for victims of Hurricane Katrina.*

But Dad, it was Leonardo, Leonardo DiCaprio! And it is for a good cause. It's only five hundred dollars. I mean I was only gonna give fifty, but when I got through, heard his voice, when he said "Hi, this is Leonardo," thought I was gonna drop my cell phone, I swear! And there I was with your credit card right there in my hand, and I thought of all those poor people in New Orleans. Well, it was like Leo put a spell on me. He talked so nice, Dad. Asked me my name. Leonardo DiCaprio asked me my name! Then we talked, and then I told him, "I'd like to donate *five hundred dollars* Mr. DiCaprio to this very worthy cause!" And you know what he said? Said, "You can call me Leo." That's what he said, thought I'd drop dead right there. "You can call me Leo." You made Leonardo DeCaprio very happy, Dad. And I'll pay you back, I promise, someday. Think of the poor kids in New Orleans. Don't be angry Dad, please.

# CHRISTINE

20s to 40s

dramatic

*Seeing Santa Claus was a terrifying*
*experience for Christine.*

I was so excited, gonna see Santa Claus! I was just four years old, and my parents were taking me to the New York City to Macy's to see . . . Well I didn't know who he was, but everybody said he was wonderful. And all the way in to the city we sang Christmas carols in the car. We got to Macy's, this big store, lots of people. Papa was holding my hand, Mama was pushing me along. Smiles, laughs. Took the crowded elevator all the way up to the top. "Going to the North Pole!" Mama smiled. And the people in the elevator laughed. When we got there, there was warm snow everywhere and colored lights and cardboard reindeer that didn't move. I was being pushed along by these little people no larger than me, *elves*. And then I saw him, this big fat man all in red! He had all this white hair, and he smiled real big and . . . And I started to scream! He was frightening! All that white and red and so fat! When he said HO! HO! HO!," and I ended up on his lap, looked up at his huge face, and then . . . then I peed all over him. Yeah, peed on Santa Claus! Mama apologized, and they whisked me away, and down in the elevator. I cried that whole elevator ride. Papa held me in his arms. When we got back in the car, no one said a word. No Christmas carols now. I had nightmares about him for weeks. And for years, I mean years, whenever I heard the words "Santa Claus," I'd pee in my pants and get real, real scared.

# CHRISTY

30s to 40s

seriocomedic

*Christy describes the date from hell*
*to her friend.*

"C'mon, give me a kiss," he said. And I said "No!"

"You got nice lips." he said.

And I said, "Take me home, please!"

And he said, "Why? C'mon, I just took you out to dinner."

"So?!" I said. "Just take me home!" And I locked my arms in protest.

But he started touching me.

And I yelled "NO!" Said, "You know what *no* means?! Means I'm not interested. Means take me the hell home!"

And you know what he did, know what he did? Opened the door, told me to get out. Said, "You know what 'walk' means? Means find your own way home, bitch!"

"You're going to just leave me here?" And he did, he left me there.

I walked a few blocks, hailed a cab, got home, and cried, just cried all night. That was it—my date. "Mr. Nice" from last night. Look, thanks for setting me up, but PLEASE, no more blind dates, okay? They're always such a disaster. At this point I'm seriously thinking of becoming a lesbian. There's just a few minor things I still need to work out. But thanks, thanks anyway.

# GINNY

20s to 30s

dramatic

*Ginny explains what it was like being
a soldier in a prison for Iraqi soldiers.*

I just did what I was told. You had to be there. Those
men, naked, chained to their beds. Their underwear covering their faces, was weird, really . . . None of 'em spoke
English. We were ordered to humiliate, break 'em down.
But inside I was thinking this is really wrong. But you do
what you're told. You make waves, you get in trouble. So
that smile you see on my face in those photos does not re-
flect what was going on inside of me. On the outside I
was laughing, yeah. But it was like I was there, but wasn't
there. Was like we were all in some crazy cartoon. And
you laugh at cartoons, right? Cartoons are funny. Well
they're even funnier when you're in them. When you *are*
the cartoon. When there's all these naked men screaming
with underwear on their faces. And you feel like you're in
some insane asylum. But you're not, no, you're in the
army. And in the army, sir, you follow orders. And I did. I
did exactly what I was told. I'm a good soldier. I follow
orders.

# STAYCE

late 20s to 40s
dramatic

*Stayce talks to a dangerous man she just
met in a bar.*

You are a bit scary, yes. When you said hello in the bar I
didn't quite know what to make of you. I mean there was
no warmth in your smile, none. You're not exactly Mr.
Nice, you know. Wasn't the smile of a guy who was being
friendly, or even trying to score. I've met those guys before. That's not you, no. And when you asked me to
come back here, well, wasn't so much an invitation as a
dare. So I'm here. I'm here on your dare . . . You're
damaged goods. Something happened to you, didn't it?
Something bad. I can tell, can see it in your eyes. You've
been through something. Well, maybe you and I have
something in common. Or maybe I just like a challenge.
Whatever. I talk too much. Turn off the lights, it's too
bright in here. I prefer it when a room is dark, pitch
black . . . Take off your clothes, go ahead. Let's get to
know each other. Turn off the light.

# ALICE

40s to 60s

seriocomedic

*Alice recalls her first date with her husband, and how they both watched Johnny Carson's first TV show.*

Johnny Carson died. Yeah, Johnny's dead, Dan. Died last night. Our first date, remember? We both watched him, Johnny. Your apartment, that small studio on West Fifty-fifth. Remember? We went to some movie and then we both watched Johnny Carson together at your apartment. Was the first time he was on *The Tonight Show*. God, he made us laugh. Was so funny! But you kept trying to feel me up, and I kept saying, "Stop it, watch the TV or I'm going!" And you stopped. And we watched Johnny. That's when I decided I really liked you, when I saw how you laughed at Johnny Carson. And then you walked me home, and I let you kiss me good night. And I went upstairs and told all my roommates all about you. And then the phone rang. Was you pretending you were Johnny Carson. Was the worst imitation ever. But we both laughed, remember? Remember? God, was a million years ago . . . Johnny Carson, God he was good.

# JEANETTE
40s to 50s
dramatic

*Jeannette tells of how she was terrified
by a stalker.*

At first I thought it was just me, that I was imagining it.
Big city, you get paranoid. But I knew, just knew someone
was following me. Felt like I was being watched all the
time. I told Herby I thought we should call the police.
"And tell them what?" he said. "That you're suspicious?"
Then he'd hold me, told me everything would be all right,
and it was. But then the phone calls started. All hours,
middle of the night. Police said there was nothing they
could do. Said he's got to make a move. I said, "What
he's gotta do, murder me?!" I was so scared, just wanted
to stay home and hide. But every night Herby would hold
me and everything would be all right. Well, finally they
caught the guy, was one of our neighbors. Then the truth
came out, he'd been paid—by Herby. Herby wanted to
bring some love back into out marriage, felt we'd drifted
apart. So he paid this guy to scare me. Police let Herby
off, said he could have got time, but they thought he had
good intentions. And now me and Herby, now we're better than ever.

# ELAINE
30s to 40s
dramatic

*Elaine tells of the life-changing realization she had while rushing to a business meeting.*

I was in the car, driving. Was rushing to a meeting this afternoon. Running late, stressed. And I was beeping at some asshole in front of me who wasn't going fast enough. Kept beeping and beeping until finally I slammed my hand hard as I could, right into the steering wheel! And I sat there in terrible pain. And while sitting there, it suddenly it dawned on me, I'm not enjoying the ride anymore. And I wasn't just thinking about the car or the guy ahead of me. I mean the ride, my life. Always needing to win a client, an appointment, whatever. I realized that I'd lost track somehow. I mean what was important . . . Look, I know I've been a monster to all of you. *(Sincerely.)* I'm sorry, I mean it, really. *(Then.)* Anyway I got off at the first exit, came home. Been sitting here for the last few hours, thinking. Just called the office, told them I quit. Maybe this is insane, but I . . . I want to start enjoying the ride again. Want to see more of you, my family, my friends. I want a life! I'm home . . . Okay, 'nuff said. So, what do you all want for dinner?

# HELENE

40s to 60s

comedic

*Helene has called her super up to her apartment to fix her stuffed pipes.*

Look, Leonardo, I'm not interested! I know you think all the women in this building are going gaga over you. Well not me, sorry. See, I don't care how sexy you are, or how great your body is. Doesn't do a thing for me. I just asked you up here to check my water heater. I wanted to take a shower, and I got cold water. That's the only reason I'm sitting here, wearing just my bathrobe. I was about to go to bed. Look, I know it's late, almost midnight, but don't read anything into that. I just needed a hot shower, I'm very tense tonight, had a rough day. So I called you, I mean you are the super. Just so you know, nothing about you turns me on. Not your tattoos, your skintight pants, nothing. And I've heard what goes on around here, oh yeah. All the trashy stories about you and how supposedly good you are in bed. Who cares? Means nothing to me! Just fix my heater and leave . . . I am now going into my bedroom, and I'm going to lie down on my big, big bed. I'll be inside waiting. Just let me know when you're ready . . . I mean finished.

# GRACE
20s to 30s
comedic

*Grace is shocked when she sees her young
children playing doctor.*

What were you two just doing? Don't look at me like
that! Don't go all shutty mouth! Mommy wants to know,
WHAT WERE YOU DOING?!

(*Softer.*) Were you playing doctor, hmm, that what
you were doing? Were you *touching* each other? That
why you're both up here hiding in the dark—like little
rats? When you touch each other like that, that's disgusting, it's *perverted*. And perverted people have to be put in
prison. And they stay there for years and years and never
get to see their Mommys or any of their friends. Those
people in prisons have snuck upstairs and touched them-
selves just like you did just now. You want to end up like
them, huh? (*A beat.*) All right, we're going to just forget
about what happened here. But we're going to make sure
it *never* happens again, right?! You wouldn't want
Mommy to have to call the police and send you to prison,
would you? . . . Now let's go downstairs like good little
boys and pray to God for forgiveness for our wicked,
wicked ways. And after we pray, Mommy will make you
a nice hot lunch.

# GINA
40s
seriocomedic

*Gina confronts a business associate.*

Jealous? Me, of you? You're kidding? That's what you think? No Bob, this is business. We're both here to make a buck. I am definitely not jealous. See, I don't like you Bob, never did. But that has nothing to do with this meeting. I got you loud and clear that first day you walked into my office with your bright white smile and over enthusiastic handshake. Your pathetic attempt at warmth told me all I needed to know. *(She looks him at him.)* Bob, I had you pegged from hello. But that's all past tense, we're with different companies now. And just because I don't like you, doesn't mean you're not invited to the party. Actually, I personally requested you for this negotiation, that's why you're even here. So just show me your paperwork and let's see if we can arrange a deal. I don't like you Bob, but I know you're a good businessman. So come, sit, talk. But keep your feelings and suspicions to yourself.

# AISHA
40s to 50s
dramatic

*Aisha tells her lawyer why she had to perform
an exorcism on a child.*

I had no choice, none. Had to save that child's soul. She
were possessed. Demons, yes. I am a good God-fearing
Christian. Christ lives within me. I praise him every day.
Wake with him in the morning and go to sleep with him
in my heart. So I would never hurt no child. Never, no.
But on that day last week, I saw all the signs. Look in her
eyes, way she spoke to me. The cursing, swearing. On
that morning that child's mouth was full of obscenities.
She thrashed about and the cursing got worse. Child had
the devil in her, I'm tellin' ya. So I knew she needed to
take a hot bath, to cleanse herself, get rid of them devils.
So I made sure that that water was hot, burning hot,
scalding. S'the only way to get them devil out. But as
hard as I tried, I could not get that child into the tub.
Those devils were more powerful than me. She went
screaming through the house, to the neighbors next door.
Next thing I knew, police were here and . . . I did nothing
wrong. I am a good God-fearing Christian. She had devils
in her, understand? Devils.

# TERESA

30s to early 40s
dramatic

*Teresa tells her husband that she has
second thoughts about having a child.*

Last night while you sleeping, I was sitting here in the
kitchen. I couldn't sleep. I was looking out the window
and realized . . . What are we doing, Ted? Bringing a
child into the world, now. The responsibility, it's too . . . !
Anyway, I got really frightened, wanted to wake you. I've
given it a lot of thought, Ted. *(Looking at him.)* I can't go
through with this. For Christ's sake, I can't even take care
of myself, let alone . . . And you, you just lost your job
and . . . I know how hard we've tried to have this baby.
How we thought it would . . . *(A beat, firmly.)* I'm going
to have an abortion. I still have a few more days left, it's
safe. Maybe I'm too selfish, I don't know. But not now.
Don't look at me like that. Please, it's for the best. Don't
look at me like that.

# RUBY
teenager
seriocomedic

*Ruby thinks about her hate
for a supposed friend.*

*(An angry inner monologue.)*
You are so transparent.
Everything you think you're hiding
                              is so obvious.
So . . . so . . . !
Do you know I can see your hate?
Hel-lo!
                    It's right there on your face—
                              in Technicolor!
And that's fine with me.
                    Because
                              I hate you, too.
I do.
And like you,
                    I've been trying
                              to hide my hate.
But it's just a waste of time.
Waste of energy.
                    We pass each other in the hall at school,
                    say hello.
But blood is dripping from your over-made-up eyes.
We both say,
                    *(Too sweetly.)* "Hi, how you doing?"
When we secretly despise each other.
Waste of time.
Waste of energy.

Wouldn't it be nice
if we could stop in the hall
and smile,
and say,
"I hate you!"
And then yell,
"And you hate me, too!"
Then calmly walk on to our next class.
*(A beat.)*
I hate your hello's.
And next time I see you,
I'll tell you so.
Actually,
I hate everything about you.
Now stick that in your ugly backpack!
*(A beat, too sweet.)* Oh, yeah, have a nice day.

# RENEE

40s

dramatic

*Renee, the wife of a celebrity, confronts him
for being inconsiderate to a friend.*

What's happened to you? He was your friend, your best
friend, have you forgotten?! We all had such good times
together. And then to treat him like he's nothing. That
was disgusting what you just did! Let me tell you something, you are using your fame as a weapon. Your boast-
ing is like a knife that you jab into people you love to
keep them away. Well, you're winning, you're succeeding
in alienating all our friends. You've become so condescending to everyone, everyone, even me. Oh you should
hear yourself sometimes. It's disgusting . . . Now I want
you to go in there and apologize to Harris and
Arlene. Almost all our friends are gone—because of you.
We haven't been invited to a dinner party in months. No
one wants anything to do with you. I'm not going to lose
Harris and Arlene too. Now you go in there and apologize. Because if you don't, I swear, I swear to God, I'm
leaving you.

# VIVIAN

## 20s
### seriocomedic

*Vivian talks about how she met Simon
Cowles of* American Idol.

It was just a moment in a corridor. Everyone else was outside. I walked in a wrong door I guess, had gotten past
security somehow. And I was getting a drink at the water
fountain. My nerves were all over the place, my mouth
was dry. Anyway, I was bending down at the faucet,
sipping some water. And when I stood up there he was.
He smiled, said, "Nice bum." Had no idea what he
meant. But then he looked at my butt, said it again,
"Nice bum." Guess it's a British word. He said, "You
here for the competition?" And I said, "Well, yes."

"My name's Simon," he said

"I know who you are, Mr. Cowles."

"So . . . would you like to come up to my room—to
relax."

"But you're a judge," I said stupidly.

"What's that got to do with anything?" he said

"Well, I don't think it's really right."

Then he stopped smiling, smirked that Simon Cowles
smirk. You know the one he always makes on TV when
he doesn't like something. And then he said, "Fine, have
it your way. Have a good day." And then he just walked
away. Rude, really rude, I thought. Thought I should tell
someone. I mean he invited me up to his room. Anyway,
when I went in to sing, he didn't even look at me.
No just looked away, which of course made me even

more nervous. I screwed up, I sucked. My voice . . . Well, I didn't get in. But I'll tell ya, I'll always wonder what would have happened if I had . . . Can't go there. Coulda, woulda, shoulda. At least now I know Simon Cowles thinks I have a nice "bum."

# HILLARY
late 20s to 30s
dramatic

*Hillary talks about her fear of being
terminally ill.*

I knew, you know? Hadn't been feeling well, was tired all
the time. I'd make breakfast, get the kids off to school,
him to work, then collapse into a chair. Stay there all day,
exhausted. So finally I made the appointment, saw the
doctor. He took tests. Few days later he called, told me to
come in. Just by the tone in his voice, I knew, I was sure.
When I sat there waiting in his office I thought, "Who'll
take care of Carl, who'll take care of the kids?" As he
came toward me, the look in his eyes, I was certain. He
started with, "I'm sorry." I looked away, wanted to cry.
But then he said, "Nothing's wrong. I think you're just
very depressed."

"Nothing's wrong, really?"

"You'll live to be a hundred, Hillary." And then he
smiled

"Let's deal with it!" Did I say that, did he? Does it
matter?

I started on the antidepressants right away, then therapy, and then, then it just lifted, the depression. And I'm
fine now, fine. *(Smiling.)* Probably live to be a hundred.

# ARLENE

Comedic

50s

*A wealthy married woman having an affair
with her tennis coach.*

*(Manic.)* It's not until you meet someone like you that
you realize how much time you've wasted. Wasted, really!
Harry was just wrong for me, I realize that now. Maybe I
married him just for the money, y'know, I don't know. I
thought it was love but . . . Maybe what we're doing
here, you and me, here in this hotel room isn't quite right,
but it doesn't feel wrong, not wrong, not at all. *(Smiling.)*
And my kids, you'll see, they'll love you, just like me.
And all that stuff I have with Harry, the condo, the
house, money, means nothing. Superficial, unimportant!
Un-im-portant! I can let go of it all in a heartbeat. And
the age thing, age thing doesn't matter, Mark! So what if
my kids are a little older than you. It's just numbers.
Mark, we can make this work! You can still teach tennis,
and I can get a job somewhere, waitress, coffee shop, I
don't care. We won't need much. What do you say?—
Honey, honey, where you going? Are you leaving?
Honey? Mark, what's wrong?!

# GWEN

30s

seriocomedic

*A company CEO engaging a man she just met at a bar.*

Strong? I don't really think in those terms. No, I don't think of myself as a *strong* woman. I know what I want, sure, of course. But doesn't everyone? Don't we all go after what we want? Don't you, Steve? The way I see myself . . . I don't know, I'm just a girl, a woman, that's all. I don't think of myself as a CEO or corporate anything. And I want, and need, like everyone else. And I saw you yesterday in the company cafeteria. You were standing on line talking to some of the guys from upstairs. And well, I liked what I saw. Thought, yeah, yes, him. But I never imagined I'd bump into you so soon, tonight, this bar. It's . . . fortuitous. Anyway, cut to the chase. I have an apartment, five minutes from here. How about coming back, a drink, my place? I'd like to get to know you better. So, what do you say? My cards are on the table, Steve . . . your call.

# RENETTE

30s to 40s
dramatic

*A desperately lonely woman reaching out
to a friend.*

I don't know, it just sort of happened, gradually. I guess I got tired all of the predictability. People can be . . . When you can finish your friend's sentences . . . It's not that I felt better than any of them, no. It's not about feeling superior. That's not what happened. I don't know, maybe I'm just too *discerning*, too picky about who I choose to spend my time with. So I started eliminating them, dropping friends. But now Anne, I find myself—isolated. Alone in a corner with no one, no friends at all. And I don't know how this happened. You are just about the only friend I have left, Anne. I need someone to help bring me back into the world, to be social again. So I'm asking for your help. This was hard, asking, believe me. But I feel so . . . so desperately alone. I don't know if there's even anything you can do, but I had to ask. It's a start. I'm reaching out, alone, and I don't want to be alone anymore.

# PATTY

30s
comedic

*A crook trying to convince her husband
to rob a bank.*

Stop bein' such a wuss, will ya? Just go in there and rob the bank. Go ahead, go, go get the money. . . . Well what are you waiting for?! C'mon, the old guard's on duty for only ten more minutes . . . What? Go! —You are such a damn coward. All right I'll do it myself. Give me the gun. Did you hear me? Give me the gun! *(He doesn't.)* You know, y'know, I thought you were such a man when I married you. You had such a swagger back then, were a real big talker. I thought you were brave. Now look at you, sittin' here, shittin' in your shoes. You're a little girl, a wuss. Afraid of some senior citizen bank guard. Give me the gun! . . . Dan, give me . . . ! *(She looks at him, alarmed.)* That's not funny. I don't like having guns aimed at me. Put the gun down. Put it . . . Dan you're starting to make me nervous, just put it down. Will you stop . . . ? Dan, put the gun down. . . . Okay, all right, we don't have to rob the bank. We can go home, have supper with the kids. You're not a wuss, okay?! I'm sorry I called . . . Dan put the gun . . . Dan . . . Put . . . Put . . . ! Please! DAN?!

# RHONDA
30s

dramatic

*A cop apologizing and tenderly saying good night to her daughter.*

Mama's sorry. Mommy just had a bad day. Now go to sleep, all right? Mama didn't mean to yell just now. Sometimes I just bring my work home, I'm sorry. There's bad people in the world, and Mommy has to catch them and put them in jail. And sometimes, well, I don't leave my anger outside. But I didn't mean to yell at you just now, I swear. You're a good girl, and I love you. And I promise from now on I'll leave my work at the precinct, okay? Now turn around, go to sleep. And tomorrow when you get up, we'll have a big breakfast and go to the zoo. *(Smiling.)* Mommy loves you; I do. Mommy loves you. See you in the morning.

# MARGIE

20s to 30s

comedic

*Margie describes the strange guy she met in
a bar the night before.*

So this guy last night, weird, but wonderful. Nice looking,
blonde, blue eyes. Tells me he's an "android," whatever
the hell that is. Figure it's some religion, y'know, like Sci-
entology or something. And he talks real slow, looks right
into my eyes. I mean how often you meet a guy in a bar
these days who's actually looking into your eyes? And he
wants to know all about me, everything. And I'm flat-
tered. So finally I say, "Hey, you want to go back to my
place?" And he says, get this, "As you wish." Well, when
we get back to my place, all I can say, was for somebody
who talked so slow, he was a freakin' sex machine! And
finally, after the FOURTH TIME, I said, "Enough al-
ready!" He looked so sad, asked if I was "displeased."
Told him no, I was just tired. When he left, I gave him my
phone number, and he *ate it*. Ate it, yeah, put it in his
mouth. Said that's how he remembers things. He was so
sweet this guy, so polite, was like from another planet.
Oh this one, this one's a keeper, a real keeper, yeah.

# HELEN

60s years old
comedic

*At sixty-eight years old, Helen finally feels to-
tally liberated.*

Because I'm sixty-eight, SIXTY-EIGHT, okay? And when
you get to be sixty-eight, son, there's a freedom that
comes with the territory. A what-the-hell, y'know?! My
whole life, I was such a goody-goody. Believed whatever
they told me; that a woman's place was always in the
backseat. I believed that crap. And I believed women's lib,
feminism, that was for the lesbians and kooks. So I stayed
home, cooked, had kids, took care of my Carl. Well now
he's gone, going on two years. And I've been living like in
a limbo, not knowing which way to go. But today, today
I am SIXTY-EIGHT! And it's never too late. So I'm buying me that bikini. That small, yellow, polka dot . . . And
y'know, y'know, I don't give a crap what people think.
And maybe I'll come back tomorrow and buy me another,
even smaller. Or one of those push up bras. Or I might
just go out to a disco, or call up some male escort service!
Have me one of them studs delivered. I might, yeah. So
wrap it up, that bikini. Put it in a box, a gift box. It's a
birthday present, from me to me. For me, a very special
lady on her sixty-eighth birthday.

# BETTE

late 20s to early 30s
dramatic

*Bette tells of her experience while running away from her wedding.*

I just got on the bus, that's all. Paid my money, got my ticket and found a seat. And that whole ride I just looked out the window, lost in terrified thoughts. Thoughts of what I had left behind. And on that bus I saw towns and rivers, all kind of places. I'd look at a house and before it could fly by I'd wonder what her life was like, the woman who lived there. Did her kids spend their Sundays in that portable pool with the dirty water? Did she and her husband have friends over for barbecues? Was she happy there in that house that needed a good painting? Or did she just stop caring? Did she start getting fat and . . . ? Had she given up everything for him? I wondered, I did. *(A beat.)* I don't know why I left him. S'no simple answer. Love him to death, I do. But it was as simple as slipping from one dress into another. Just got on the bus heading for points unknown. Disappear—for better or worse. Forever, till death . . . Well forever's too long! Please, don't look at me like that. I'm so sorry, for everything, all the trouble I've . . . I'm back now, I'm back. And that's all that matters, isn't it?

# VERNICE
30s to 50s

seriocomedic

*Vernice describes her naughty dream in which George Clooney is her dentist.*

And so I had this dream. And in it George Clooney was my dentist. George Clooney! And George, he tells me I have halitosis. And I'm terribly embarrassed. I mean here I have bad breath with George Clooney, couldn't ya die? But then, in my dream, Brad Pitt walks in. Brad Pitt! And he's wearing white. He's the dental hygienist. He's there to *sweeten* my breathe, he says. And Brad smiles that cute Brad Pitt smile, and then puts his sexy hand deep into my mouth. And in my dream I happen to notice that Brad don't have no gloves on, no latex gloves. And I'm thinkin', "Aren't they supposed to wear gloves? He shouldn't be puttin' his hands in people's mouths with no gloves on." But then I think, "Well what the hell, it's Brad Pitt!" And besides, George is standing right next to him. And George is smiling at me, that sexy, comforting . . . So I let Brad put his fingers, his whole hand, deep, deep into my mouth. And it felt *so* good having his hand in there. And best of all I know that when he's through I will no longer have halitosis. My breath will smell like sweet summer roses. And his hand's going deeper and deeper, deeper and deeper! And I don't even gag on it or any-thing, no . . . But then, then I wake up, open my eyes. And I realize I'm home in bed with Harry. And he's on top of me. A little sneak attack while I was asleep. And his breath, my God, horrible, halitosis. I quickly close my eyes hoping I'll see Brad or George! But there's only Harry, only Harry, Harry.